Amanda Theodocia Jones

Ulah

And Other Poems

Amanda Theodocia Jones

Ulah
And Other Poems

ISBN/EAN: 9783744653022

Printed in Europe, USA, Canada, Australia, Japan

Cover: Foto ©Thomas Meinert / pixelio.de

More available books at **www.hansebooks.com**

ULAH,

AND

OTHER POEMS.

BY
AMANDA T. JONES.

SECOND EDITION.

BUFFALO:
H. H. OTIS,
AND
BREED, BUTLER & CO.
1861.

Entered according to Act of Congress, in the year 1866

BY REV. RUFUS COOLEY, JR.,

In the Clerk's Office of the District Court for the Northern District of New York.

C. E. FELTON,
STEREOTYPER AND PRINTER
BUFFALO, N. Y.

J. M. JOHNSON,
Printer and Binder,
BUFFALO, N. Y

TO MY FATHER,

WHO, FOR MORE THAN SIX YEARS, HAS JOYFULLY
HEARD THE HARPS OF THE BLESSED;

AND MY MOTHER,

WHO, TARRYING YET, KINDLY LISTENS TO THE FAINT, PRELUDING STRAINS
OF MY OWN LITTLE HARP,

THESE HUMBLE SONGS

ARE LOVINGLY INSCRIBED,

BY THE AUTHOR.

CONTENTS.

Preface,	7
Ulah,	9
Reign of Truth,	91
Hide and Seek,	94
Peace,	98
Locust Leaves,	100
Glen Elgin,	105
Reminiscences,	108
A Chick-a-dee Song,	111
A Song for Reformers,	114
The Silver Chalice,	118
Charity,	121
Waiting,	123
The King of the North,	125
The Child, the Maiden, the Mother,	128
The Tide of Life,	135
The Laboring Man,	138
Dream Land,	143
Dewdrops of Knowledge,	146
Life's Warfare,	148
The Wind,	152
Parting,	155
The Price of Blood,	158
The Willow Tree,	161
Nature's Feast,	163
Our Playmate's Grave,	165
The Music of the Soul,	167
The Christening,	170

CONTENTS.

OH! WOULD I WERE ALONE,	173
PRAYER AND PRAISE,	175
THE DYING TEACHER,	177
SONG,	182
THE FLOWER LANGUAGE OF THE HEART,	184
THE BIRD AND THE HEART,	189
THE INVALID'S DREAM,	191
THE THREE BIRDLINGS,	196
HAPPY DAYS,	205
LIGHT,	207
THE MESSENGER,	211
WHO KNOWETH THE HEART,	213
THE DEATH OF THE OLD YEAR,	215
HEAVEN,	218
THE LESSON,	220
VISIONS,	223
THE FUTURE,	226
TO A LITTLE POETESS,	228
MOTHER NATURE,	230
THE STORY OF A WRONGED LIFE,	232
THE HIDDEN FOUNTAIN,	235
THE TRANSPLANTED FLOWER,	238
TO JENNIE K——,	240
A HYMN OF DEITY,	243
AND BEHOLD! IT WAS GOOD,	246
CAROLINE,	249
SPRING WINDS,	252
THE WORLD,	255
THE SOUL'S TRIUMPH,	259
A WINTER IN SPRING,	264
SUMMER,	267
IF,	270
MY SPIRIT LUTE,	272
A PHANTASY,	275
BELL,	278
SNOW BERRIES,	280
THE DEAD PINE,	291

PREFACE.

I have known a few spring flowers, brought by the hand of a feeble child, kindle flashes of feeling in the face of the sternest man: so, neither fearing undue censure, nor deprecating just criticism, I lay my little offering before the public, hoping that, like a bouquet of early blossoms, it will serve to remind some earth-worn soul of the freshness and fragrance of its happy May. A. T. J.

ULAH:

AN INDIAN LEGEND VERSIFIED.

ULAH.

PROEM.

Oh! if the rocks on which we tread
Could gather back the sounds long dead,
And crowd our ears with each wild tale,
How would the gayest spirit quail!

Beneath this low stone's quiet face,
Some spade has dug a burial-place;
Beside that boulder in the wood,
Some hand has spilled a brother's blood.

The half-breathed curse, the sudden blow,
The gurgling sound of dying woe,
The stifled moan, the panting breath,
As some scared victim strove with death.

Perchance, all these, in bygone hours,
Have rocked the air and bowed the flowers;
Have smote the rocks with viewless rod,
And echoed in the ear of God.

There towers a rock in the far west,
Whose hapless history is guessed:
A story sweet as summer gale,
Yet mournful as an autumn wail.

Each mossy crevice drips with tears,
Through all the sunny, laughing years,
As if its flinty heart were wrung
With fears untold and woes unsung.

Through all the day, delirious calls
Sink to the ground in fitful falls;
Through all the night, strange shadows fly,
And spectral faces glimmer by.

It may be but the songs of birds,
That seem to drop below in words;
It may be but the firs' unrest,
Or moonbeams, glancing from its breast;

But, still, beside it, sudden dread
Will turn aside the bravest head;
And, still, the heart, with hurried beat,
Quickens the fall of passing feet.

List to the tale. A dying race
Claims for its legends kindly place.
Let the heart-throb of olden time
Pulse onward through the veins of rhyme.

And if the voice, that in your ear
Sings this wild tale of love and fear,
Be weak, unmusical, forgive;
But let the simple story live.

CANTO I.

When royal, sun-descended Spring
Had made the beggar world a king;
Had softly warmed his frozen veins,
And washed him clean in balmy rains;
Had 'broidered robes of changeful green,
His wintry nakedness to screen;
Had starred his breast with flowers white,
And crowned his brow with bands of light,
Oconee, in his swift canoe,
Flung from his oar the river dew,
As lightly as a bird might fling
The raindrops from his rapid wing.

Alone and peaceful, gliding far
Toward the beauteous morning star,
His birchen bark, through forests deep,
Stemmed the slow waters' winding sweep,
Loitered where prairie-grasses gave
Their slight reflections to the wave,

And stole, with graceful curve, away
From flower-gemmed isle and mimic bay.

Through many a lone and starry night,
It held its dark, untiring flight;
With the fleet west-wind swept along,
And woke the wave to louder song.
The insects' call, the tinkling sweet
Of the light brooklet's dancing feet,
The oft-repeated mandate shrill
Of passion's bird — the whippowil —
All evening voices, soft and clear,
Made music in the Indian's ear.

The crescent, to a half-moon grown,
Her smile above the world had thrown,
And dipped the wave with silver bowl,
Ere he had reached his secret goal.
But, 'neath the early morning star,
He smiled to see, in distance far,
The ragged rocks' familiar face,
That marked for him a resting-place.

Up the dim east the sunbeams flew,
And lightly, faintly quivered through

Cerulean space, as wonders rise,
And light a new-born infant's eyes.
How beautiful the morning seemed!
How fair the bubbling ripples gleamed,
That lifted up their ermined edges,
And crowned with foam the drooping sedges!

The light Miami-mist arose,
Like one from healthful, cool repose;
And, opening her azure eyes,
Looked drowsily toward the skies.
The red baneberry's white-flowered boughs
Shook 'neath the gray rocks' mossy brows;
The red-bud, in the bright-robed wood,
Smiled o'er the mandrake's flaunting hood;
And the huge plane-tree, by the wave,
Stood, like a warrior, strong and brave;
And, waving far his long, white limbs,
Sang to the clouds his battle-hymns.

The graceful doe, toward the brink,
Led down her slender fawn to drink;
The meadow-lark arose and flung
The flute-like matins from his tongue;
The red-winged blackbird, hurrying out

From the high reedmace, joined the shout;
And thousand slender, arching throats
Cast to the wind their gleeful notes.

Oconee's was a savage soul;
Yet did his crimson pulses roll
With sudden swell, beneath the power
That wakened bird, and tree, and flower,
To beautify the golden hour.

So softly splendid, and so new
Rose the fair world into the view,
It seemed as if some secret power,
Alladin-like, in midnight hour,
Had but commanded, and swift hands
Had silver-barred the hidden lands—
Had garlanded a palace hall,
And reared a curtained dome o'er all;
Had strewn with diamonds every street,
Some happy princess-bride to greet.

Oconee saw, and stayéd his oar,
To see the glad day upward soar,
Till the last ripple that the blade,
With free and wing-like sweep, had made,

Melted, and just a thread-like gleam
Told where his bark had cleft the stream.

And "Oh!" he thought, "If death can bring
A brighter day, a sweeter spring;
If fairer hunting-grounds can lie,
Blooming, beyond the shining sky,
Then were it very good to die."

Suddenly, all the air around
Was shaken by a tide of sound,
That, swollen full, and interwound
With resonant murmurs, floated near
In viewless billows, till the ear,
Bewildered with the silver throng,
Knew not the echoes from the song.
It floated near;—with glowing face,
With blithesome step, and form all grace,
With glance as bright as sunrise beam,
An Indian maiden sought the stream.

Her arm was like the willow bough;
Like night's first cloud, her dusky brow;
Her lips like summer's scarlet flowers,
Moist with the dew-fall's misty showers.

Like the grape's clinging tendrils, wound
Over the ripe fruit, full and round,
Close to her cheek her tresses trailed,
And half its beauty darkly vailed.

But oh, her voice!—as if the breeze
Had gathered all rich melodies,
And, deftly mingling them, had found
Her lips its medium of sound!
A tremor of the chant that breaks,
When th' ice-fettered stream awakes
In sunny spring to its new joys—
The waterfall's glad, babbling noise,
The sound of boughs by light winds stirred,
The clearest song of woodland bird,
The madrigals the wild bees sing,
The rustle of the hum-bird's wing;
All these, with rare, artistic choice,
Seemed blended in the maiden's voice.

Oconee heard, and to the shore
He plied his light and muffled oar,
Over the tufted grasses stole,
To hear the nearer numbers roll,

And when the last sweet echo died,
Had softly neared the maiden's side.

One slight foot planted in the flood,
With graceful drooping head, she stood,
To see the streaming of her hair,
In raven lines, reflected there,
But started, with a sudden frown,
To see another face look down,
And turned, with angry haste, to see
Who might this bold intruder be.

Oconee's form was straight and fine,
As is the stately forest pine.
A chieftain's mantle girt his breast;
A snowy feather was his crest;
His blazing eye was clear and bright,
As is the glowing, midday light,
Yet kindly as the sleeping stream
That sparkles back the nitid beam;
And, when he spoke, his voice was like
The voice of billows, when they strike
O'er hidden rocks, and onward go,
Sinking away in tuneful flow.

"And does the maiden frown," he said,
"Because a warrior's step is led
Toward her, as the thirsty fawn
Seeks the clear stream when night is gone?
Must wrathful thoughts her dark eyes light,
As fire-flies flash in summer night,
Because a brother hopes to find
A friendly smile, a greeting kind?
When the bright spring-birds sing their lays,
The smiling waters melt in praise;
The warrior's heart is brave and strong,
But melted at the maiden's song."

"And who art thou?" she shyly said,
With downcast eye, and drooping head;
"Ulah is very young and weak;
Why does the brave his sister seek?"

"I am Oconee. Far away
From the red clouds of setting day,
I come to seek, beside the wave,
For Shabbonah's neglected grave.
He was my sire, a chieftain great,
Whose brave heart was the eagle's mate,
To all he loved, as good and kind,

As the low-talking, pleasant wind;
But like the tempest, that lays low
The highest trees, amid the foe.

"He had been wronged: From far he came
To bring his enemy to shame.
Pauwega heard his warriors shout,
And sent a poisoned arrow out,
That pierced and smote him to the ground.
In the still night, we gathered round
To hear his death-song; then we made
A grave beneath a rock's deep shade,
And to his rest the chief we laid.

"Shall Shabbonah, in his lone bed,
Struck by the foe's unwitting tread,
By friend nor son be visited?
Shall his great spirit mourning go,
Shamed with neglect and weighed with woe?
Not while Oconee's arm can guide
His swift canoe along the tide;
Though thousand moons between us sweep,
Oconee, at his grave, would weep."

Oh! when did woman ever hear

A tale like this nor shed a tear
Of tender sympathy! the world
Has many deep clouds o'er it furled;
But on the darkest mist there lies
The pitying light of woman's eyes.

And "Oh!" the maiden cried, "but show
To Ulah where he slumbers low,
And she will rear above the dead
The purple cone-flower's lofty head;
And o'er the red-root's clustering charms,
Will wind the moon-seeds' slender arms;
The blazing star and blooming feather
Shall lay their talking lips together,
And tell how, like a warrior great,
Oconee's father met his fate.

"When the sun's wigwam in the west
Lets the bright chieftain in to rest;
While its red doors are open wide,
Then Shabbonah's brave soul will glide
From that far hunting-ground's white shore,
To see his lonely grave once more;
And every flower that waves above
Shall whisper of Oconee's love."

The savage turned his grateful look
Full on the maiden, till she shook
With bashful heart-pulsations stirred,
Like the twig swayed by startled bird.

"My sister has a loving heart,"
He murmured, as she drew apart,
And screened from his warm eyes her cheek,
That softly flamed to hear him speak.
"My sister's words are sweet and good,
Like rains that drop within the wood;
Her looks are like the rainbow, bowed
In brightness on the summer cloud.

"Once, when the chieftain's years were few,
Within his father's wigwam grew
A little, slender, maiden form,
Whose heart, with tender love, was warm.
Oh! she was graceful as the fawn;
Her smile was like the smile of dawn;
Her face was like the new moon, white,
Half folded in the clouds of night.
And, still, her step grew soft and slow;
And, still, her voice grew weak and low;
And, still, with every moon, she grew

Whiter and whiter in our view.
When sixteen springs had o'er her fled,
Owaissa slept among the dead.

"When the loud thunders roll around,
The broken maize-stalk smites the ground;
So sunk the warrior's broken heart,
To see his sister's soul depart.
And he has sought her grave and prayed,
At earliest dawn, to meet her shade;
Has piled the purple prairie flowers
Above her head, in summer hours;
And, with wet face, has sought the skies,
To see Owaissa's starry eyes.

"None love Oconee. He is young;
But early grief has stilled his tongue.
When all his noisy warriors go
To chase the herded buffalo,
He flings his arrows out with skill,
But thinks upon Owaissa still.

"When the sun rose to-day, he felt
His icy sorrow in him melt;
And thought, ere this bright day had passed,

To see his sister's soul at last;
And, when he heard the maiden's tongue,
He deemed it was Owaissa sung;
And knew not but his soul had found
The warrior's happy hunting ground."

Ulah had listened to the tale
With dewy eyes, and face all pale;
But, when the last sad word had died,
Up from her heart the crimson tide
Floated, until her cheek's soft bloom
Rivaled the rosebay's purple plume.

Like the slow wind at sunset, came
Her low reply. She breathed his name,
And whispered, "If my brother will,
Ulah will be Owaissa still."

———

Oh love! omnipotent and high!
One soft glance of a soul-full eye,
With but *another* glance agreeing,
Can call you into endless being.
One little touch of clasping hands
Will bind your precious, golden bands,

That time, nor woe, nor death can sever—
Love, living once, lives on forever;
And never yet a spirit grew
To rare completeness, if the dew
Of some sweet love, with sacred power,
Crept not within, and fed the flower.

CANTO II.

The mild, soft, Indian-summer day
Moved dreamily along her way,
Like one, accustomed long to woe,
Who feels again love's genial flow;
Yet, burden'd with the tide's excess,
Finds it too heavenly-sweet to bless.

Her regal garment's purple fold
Was tinged with green, and edged with gold,
And silvery mist, like gleaming lace,
Vailed the soft splendor of her face.

Oh! had ye heard her rustling tread,
As o'er the yellow leaves she sped,
By calm October kindly led,
Ye would have sought her queenly side,
As those who cluster round a bride,
Too solemn in their hearts to smile,
Yet wondrous joyful all the while.

O'er the broad western land she went,
And all the trees obsequious bent;
Their golden leaves before her cast,
And sang her praises, as she passed.
The brooks, beneath the shimmering sheet
Her hand had flung across their feet,
Lay tranced and silent, yet astir,
As if in sleep they dreamed of her.

All gemmed with rains, and softly bright,
The grassy prairie charmed the sight;
And, tossed in waves by every breeze,
Chanted its laughing melodies,
While, through it, like a silver street,
Shone the clear river, broad and fleet,
And traced anew each tinted cloud,
That o'er its azure face was bowed;
And here and there, along its side,
The gorgeous groves stood, many-dyed,
And laughing softly, in reply,
Whispered their joy to earth and sky.

The lime-grass thrust its lances up
Beside the aster's fringed cup;
The splendid sunflower, toward the east,
Bowed his bright head, like Jewish priest;

The purple-flowered ironweed
Towered darkly o'er the sighing reed;
And the fair self-heal smiled beneath
The turgid thistle's downy sheath;
While, like a heart, all bare and cold,
When life's glad summer showers its gold,
Awakening into blooming life,
When sorrow's darkening clouds are rife,
The wild witch-hazel held aloft
Its flowers, like golden starbeams soft.
All merrily, the glad time through,
Echo, on argent pinions, flew;
And, caroling with wondrous art,
Made even discord touch the heart.

Yet, when the sun was lost to view,
And mist was gathering into dew,
There rose so wild, so sweet a lay,
That even Echo, in dismay,
Scarce dared repeat the gushing song,
Lest she should do the minstrel wrong.

'T was like the tune that fancy sings
When we have dreamed of holy things;
'T was like the full, rich songs of birds,
Save that it melted into words.

Oh! the world, like a chief, wears his blanket of red,
And the clouds, like white feathers, wave over his head;
Bright pleasure and plenty have gladdened his sway,
And his wigwam is warm with the smiles of the day.

I saw her come out of her dwelling afar,
When there stood in the east but one beautiful star;
Like the corn-silk her tresses were over her cast,
And her moccasins scattered white beads, as she passed.

Five times has the old moon forgotten to glow,
Five times has she bent in the darkness her bow,
Since thou, my Oconee, didst sing in my ear,
And the river leaped up in its gladness to hear.

While we sat by the place where the oak stands alone,
And his heavy, green mantle was over us thrown,
Thou saidst, when five full moons have brightened the shade,
The chief will wait here for the sweet-singing maid.

All day has my fond heart been sounding thy praise,
While I plucked, with the maidens, the ripe, yellow maize;
I prayed the Great Spirit to grant me a sign,
And, lo! as we husked them, the red ears were mine.[a]

Thine eye is like lightning in darkness that shines;
Thy voice like the strong wind that roars through the pines;
Thy words like smooth arrows that leap from the quiver;
Thy crest like the white foam that gleams on the river.

I have dreamed in the night of thy fair western home;
Unstring thy bent bow, let the prairie-wolf roam.
We will follow the river that sings while it flies;
We will pass to the west like the stars in the skies.

The warrior, to his promise true,
Had waited since the day was new,
Where, swollen, with autumnal rains,
Swept the fair river of the plains.[b]

With wily glance, as one who knows
Each mound may hide revengeful foes,
Ere yet the early shades had shrunk,
He climbed the burr-oak's ragged trunk.
Thick were the boughs, the foliage dense;
Deep in the center, parting thence
The red-leaved limbs to either side,
His supple form he sought to hide.[c]

Scarce was its rustling head at rest,
Ere tumult shook his Indian breast:
From the far eastern wood came out
The clangor of a sudden shout;
And many a brave, with crimson crest,
With naked limbs, and painted breast,
Came o'er the plain with footstep fleet,
To scare the wolf from his retreat.[d]

Ne-pow-ra led them — Ulah's sire —
A chief whose lightest hate was dire,

Whose eye was like the firelight flash,
Whose limbs were lithe as mountain ash.

Why starts the hidden chieftain so?
Ne-pow-ra is his deadliest foe,
And he would bear, for vengeance sake,
The hottest fires that light the stake;
Would smile to see the warriors swarm,
Exulting, round his writhing form,
Could he but still, with fatal dart,
The rapid current of that heart.

Yet lifts he not his bended bow;
But, with stern features, whispers low
"He loves his daughter, let him go;
How fierce will be his wrath to know
She leaves her father for a FOE!

How slight an influence will control
That wayward thing, the human soul!
Just as it trembles at the goal
Of all it most has wished or sought,
A sudden lightning-blaze of thought
Will burn its straw-like schemes to nought.
Touched by the tremble of a tone
That rings responsive to its own;

Swayed by a sign, a smile, a word,
That leads it like a silken cord;
Its largest purpose passes by
As lightly as a zephyr's sigh.

Oconee's hatred had been nursed
Within his baby breast, at first;
From his young lips the shout had burst
That bade Ne-pow-ra be accursed.
When Shabbonah, with dying breath,
Had sung his boasting song of death,
And all his braves stood mourning by
To see their haughty chieftain die,
His son had sworn to fight the foe,
Till his last warrior slumbered low.

Oconee's hate was fierce and fell;
But Ulah's love had bound him well;
And hardly can revenge and love
Together o'er the heart-chords move.

As the young dawn grew full and round,
The tangled maze of dreamy sound,
The quietude but half at rest,
The soft blaze on the river's breast,
The solitude that seemed to wind

A strange, weird glamour o'er the mind,
Mingled with thoughts of Ulah's smile,
Served the young chieftain's heart to wile
From every vengeful purpose wild,
And changed the savage to a child.

When the broad, blazing sun was high,
Alone, Ne-pow-ra wandered by;
Yet little did Oconee care
To smite him, from his leafy lair;
And had the two together stood,
A word, agreeing with his mood,
Had quenched for aye his thirst for blood,
And sealed the bond of brotherhood.

———

Upon the night-clouds' broken line,
The red-winged rays of daylight shine,
Then flutter, down, like birds to rest,
And slumber in the dusky west.

The evening, like a timid maid,
Blissful, but coy and half afraid,
Following the warrior-planet, Mars,
Lifts her vailed face among the stars.

So, o'er the prairie, Ulah draws,
With lingering step and frequent pause,
Singing, because her happy breast
Can no way let the echo rest.
With startled glance, subdued and shy,
Trembling to meet her lover's eye,
She nears the burr-oak's branches dense,
With noisy heart and 'wildered sense.

As morning's hands the shades divide
That banner all the heavens wide,
So from his lair Oconee starts,
And the dark foliage gayly parts;
Leaps earthward, as the eagle darts,
With sudden downward swoop, to meet
His Ulah's light and loitering feet.

If love but flamed within the breast,
Where all wild passions are at rest,
Then were it but a comet train,
With sudden light to smite the brain,
And pass away, unfruitful, vain,
Leaving the soul to night again.

But love is like the sun's broad smile,
And can be hidden but awhile

By passion's densest clouds; they pass,
And in the soul their blackness glass;
But, when their huge, cold wings depart,
The sunlight permeates the heart.

The youthful chief had felt the fire
That leaps from murderous desire.
Like the wild horse, by envy spurred,
To strive for mastery of the herd,
He had gone forth to meet the foe,
With blood for blood and blow for blow;
But now, beneath a maiden's look,
His heart was like the midday brook,
That carols through a shining meadow,
Undarkened by the lightest shadow.

Few were his words, and but expressed
To still the tumult of his breast;
Bending his face to meet her cheek,
Barely the wind could hear him speak.

"Oconee's heart has longed for thee,
As the white summer longs to see
The first bright flowers, that shake all over,
To meet the burning sun — their lover.

Where the great, sleepy river stirs,
My couch is spread with softest furs;
And, where yon distant thicket waves,
They wait for thee — my patient braves."

Away, beside the rolling river,
Where wave-tossed foam-beads whitely quiver
And frightened flowers peer down and shiver,
They pass, and leave the world to yearn,
In tender tears, for their return.

For their return;— Oh! long shall night
Vail, with wild tears, her blinding sight;
Long shall the foam-beads gild the wave,
That dies with passion, but to lave
The restless feet that once flung back
Its waters from their pebbled track;
Long shall the plaintive winds awake
And breathe a wail for Ulah's sake;
Long shall the blue sky, leaning o'er,
Look for the BEAUTIFUL once more,
Ere she shall soothe their yearning pain,
Or dower them with her songs again.

The flower fades, the dew exhales,
The purple light of dawning pales,

ULAH.

The sweet moon dies, the breaking cloud
Wraps the white star as in a shroud,
The very wind, that leaps with mirth,
Lags, and lies dead upon the earth;
And maidens, fair as Ulah, lay
Their beauties underneath the clay.

It is but meet; for good must fill
The darkest consequences still;
And even death may yield a bliss
As sacred as a lover's kiss.

CANTO III.

Low in the west the sun had set,
And night, with starry coronet,
Bent down, her ebon hand to lay
Upon the flashing eyes of day.

The moonbeams, pallid and aslant,
Crept thro' the wildwood's darkened haunt;
Laid their white fingers here and there,
As half in blessing, half in prayer;
Brightened each tall tree's faded crest,
And left in shadow all the rest.

But, in the forest's deepest glade,
A wilder light dispelled the shade;
Glared through the gilded dark, and made
The famished panther flee afraid.

It was Ne-pow-ra's council fire,

Sending its broad blaze high and higher,
Even as the fierce, avenging ire
Burned in the breast of Ulah's sire.

It leaped along the drifting smoke,
Dividing night with sudden stroke;
Swept o'er translucent leaves, that grew
Red as the light that pierced them through;
Then, rushing from the forest, flew
To gild with flame the prairie dew.

The owl, astir, grew still again,
Winked at the blaze with sudden pain;
Then raised her cumbrous wings, and swept
Where, undisturbed, the shadows crept.
The partridge, (wont to sleep at night,)
Awakened at the bursting light,
Disturbed within his low retreat,
His long and rolling measure beat,
Even as a warlike drummer might
When heralding approaching fight.

A hundred little voices woke,
And the night's quiet slumber broke;
A bough's low murmur of dismay,

As its last leaves were borne away;
The plaintive sob of many a rill,
That told its grief to vale and hill;
A broken sound from every glen,
Like whispered words of guilty men;
All seemed to say this evening hour
Was fraught with deathful, murderous power.

Ne-pow-ra in his wigwam stood,
And mused alone in bitter mood.
Where were the bounding feet that wont
To meet him coming from the hunt?
Where was the arm that used to wind
About his neck, that love might find
Swift ingress to his clouded mind?
Where was the hand that used to clasp,
With pressure light, his larger grasp,
Then haste, with gentle touch and kind,
His deerskin moccasins to bind?
Where were the eyes, so warm and soft,
That soothed his savage humor oft;
The voice that sung, at eventide,
Wild songs, that fed his vaulting pride,
Of battle fought and valor tried?

Quenched was the hearth-fire's ruddy blaze;

No hand to crush the golden maize;
No face to beam with tender care;
He dwelt alone with silence there.

Oh! what are all the baubles worth
That deck the kingly sons of earth —
Honor, and wealth, and pride of birth,
If warmth has died upon the hearth;
If the light, falling from the skies,
Leap never back from kindly eyes;
If the wind-waves, that idly rove,
Divide not with the breath of love.

Terrific, as the chieftain stood,
Was the still fury of his mood;
That, drowning all his spirits good,
Grew madly clamorous for blood;
When, thro' his doorway, streamed the light
That flung such challenge to the night.

Oh! had the youths delayed awhile,
To light the huge and ready pile,
A gentler mood had come, perchance,
And dimmed the lightning of his glance,
As, when the fire-king's armies bound

Within the forest's shuddering ground,
The clouds along the heavens drift,
And stay the ruin, dire and swift;
So memories had o'er him flown
Of the dear lost one's look and tone,
Of filial, fond affection shown,
And pardoning tears, like blessed rain,
Had quenched the flames within his brain.

But shall the braves in council meet,
And wait Ne-pow-ra's idle feet?
When the wild war-fires climb and curl,
Shall *they* their dread defiance hurl,
And *he* be silent as a girl?
He waits no more — his heart is strong
To plan swift vengeance for its wrong.
From his low door, with footstep bold,
As haughtily as e'er of old,
He leaps, like wind along the waves,
And stands among his gathered braves.

Never saw night a scene so near
Like Hades' lurid realms of fear:
A stifling smoke arose and spread,
In raven blackness, overhead;

The raging flames, with furnace breath,
Like brothers warring to the death,
Flung their red swords, now left, now right,
In ruthless, battling haste to smite.
With faces gleaming like a host
Of demon men and angels lost,
A thousand stalwart forms were bowed
Beneath the upward-winging cloud.
Back from the scene, the circling night
Fled with a strange, uncertain flight;
Then paused, and, daring to look back,
Stood chained with terror in her track;
A blackness here — a fire-wreath there —
The roar of flames through all the air;
The dropping down of smitten bough;
The warrior's high and awful vow;
The flash of woman's curious gaze;
(Alas! that *woman's* eye should blaze
With eager joy, when vengeance waits
To leap from out his blood-stained gates!)
And worse, immeasurably worse,
The sound of childhood's lisping curse,
All these, combining, seemed to make
The very trees with terror quake.
Then, like a lightning-blasted pine,

That scorns his kingship to resign,—
Albeit the green, imperial crown
From his proud head hath fallen down,—
The chieftain towered above the throng,
And told the story of his wrong.

"Warriors," he said, "and brothers, hear!
Ye know Ne-pow-ra can not fear;
And would the eagle meekly rest,
To see the horn'd owl rob his nest?
Last night the moon was round and white;
And Nain-dee, hunting by its light,
Saw Ulah o'er the prairie go,
And, following her footsteps slow,
He heard her love-song faintly fly,
On echo-wings, toward the sky;
Saw where her coward-lover broke,
The branches of the river-oak;
And when the warrior nearer drew,
Oconee's panther-face he knew.

"With whispered words, as those afraid
Beneath the tree awhile they stayed;
Then, by the river's sighing breast,
They passed together toward the west.

"Shall this vile foe unpunished stalk,
With laughing eye and bragging talk,
And say, 'Ne-pow-ra's anger gnaws,
His breast, but he must idly pause,
For all his trembling braves are squaws?'"

He spoke as one who scorned his theme,
Then sat him down, as if the stream
Of wrath, that o'er his senses beat,
Had passed, and swept him from his feet.

Pauwega rose: 'neath his bent brows,
An eye flashed out whose glance could rouse
The dullest warrior's heart, and streak,
With instant glow, his swarthy cheek.
Majestic, yet uncouth, he stood,
Like rugged oak-tree in the wood;
And on his arms, and o'er his breast,
His giant sinews lay at rest,
Swollen out from the surface round,
Like huge roots clamb'ring o'er the ground.
His voice, at first was low and light,
Then rising in a bolder flight,
Rang through the wood, so loud and clear,
That the high tree-tops rocked to hear;
Never discordant, never sharp;

But like a full, resounding harp,
When skillful fingers deftly fling,
Grand, martial numbers from each string,
Kept still a little underswell,
Like the faint echo of a knell;
And, in its highest eloquence,
Came *subtly softened* to the sense.

"Brothers, the chieftain's heart is sore;
Love lights his silent home no more;
Like this tall tree, his head grows old,
Already is his wigwam cold.

"The winds of winter, sharp and swift,
Will pile around the snowy drift;
And who shall build the fire, to warm,
At night, Ne-pow-ra's freezing form?

"All day he looked to see the face,
Where brightness made its dwelling-place;
All day he sat in grief, alone,
Because his singing bird had flown.

"My brothers, who is this that comes,
With crafty step into our homes,

And bears away, toward the west,
Our fairest flower upon his breast?

"Oconee, son of that far foe,
Who at our hearts three springs ago,
Aimed his swift darts, and sought to tear
From our high heads the raven hair!

"Pauwega's heart grew hot to hear,
Their bragging war-songs smite his ear;
From his strong bow the arrow fled,
And Shabbonah bowed down his head.

"He came, like river strong and fleet;
Stern as the rocks we stood to meet;
And, as the cataract's waters pour,
He fell, and sleeps forevermore.

"Shall the snake's offspring dare to rise,
And with the eagle sweep the skies?
Soar through the clouds, and tell the sun
What deeds his crawling sire has done?

"Saying, 'The mighty chieftain made
Ne-pow-ra's haughty band afraid,
And I, Oconee, came from far,
And bore away his brightest star?'

"Let the broad west cry out in shame,
And let the south grow bright with flame!
Let the keen east wind swiftly blow,
And northern tempests answer, 'No!'

"Arise! Let us, like storm winds strong,
Follow these flying leaves along,
While our swift arrows, in the wind,
Sing, like the trees we leave behind.

"Arise! and let the forest hear
Our warcry bursting loud and clear,
While the dumb rocks shall voiceful grow,
And echo, 'Vengeance on the foe!'"

Strong as the hurricanes that sweep,
And tear up billows from the deep,
His words rushed out; and all the braves
Leaped answering up like howling waves,—
Gestured their fierce desires, and cried
For WAR, to cover wounded pride,
Till, roused to fury, all the throng,
By savage impulse dire and strong,
Tossed their red arms, like flames, about,
And sent their wildest war-cry out.

Back came the howling notes, increasing,
New sounds from pregnant echo leasing;
Along the wild wood arches darting,
To lone and distant haunts departing,
A hundred horrid voices yelling,
And hundred rocks the tones repelling —
Dying, returning, sinking, swelling,
Till the last echo found a dwelling,
Where rivulet bells their chimes were knelling,
And sobbed away her latest breath,
Locked in the stifling arms of Death.

Ah! now Ne-pow-ra's arm could lead
A thousand braves to do the deed
Of speedy vengeance! — for the hate
That at the *heart* its thirst must sate,
Once roused, no cooling, silver flood
Can quench the hot desire for blood.
When once some mischief-loving hand
Flings out the little burning brand
Into the prairie, a faint shine
Will mark its course, and then a line
Along the ground will redly gleam,
Like sunset ray along the stream;
Then a still blaze, and then at length

A sudden rousing into strength;
As if, like a wild battle steed,
The pawing flame were urged to speed,
On — on — along the ground it flies,
While the smoke-clouds like dust arise!
On — on to battle — while the wind
Lashes its sounding whip behind!
No angry shout — no loud command —
But while the surge rolls o'er the land
A sound through all the wide air peals,
As if of thousand chariot wheels;
And fiery hosts, like ambushed men,
Leap up from every pleasant glen.
Westward and northward, near and far
Rushes the elemental war;
And louder yet the muffled sound
Rides rumbling o'er the trampled ground,
Till all along the grassy way
Death riots on his smitten prey,
Robs the sweet plain of all its bloom,
And makes the world one vaulted tomb.
Thus, thus the little burning dart
Was sent into Ne-pow-ra's heart;
And thus the silent crimson glow
Crept slowly, wavering to and fro,
Till bursting hotly from its rest,

It kindled every savage breast,
And woke a fire that could not die,
Till it had blackened earth and sky,—
Till the sweet flowers that used to bless
Were shriveled into nothingness.

CANTO IV.

An hour went by;—the brightening moon
Waved her white robe the world aboon,
And swept the misty vail aside
From her calm face, like a young bride
That leans to hear her bridegroom speak,
With tranquil eyes and heart-pale cheek.

Oh, earth! so beautiful when noon
Prints splendors with her flaming shoon
So sweetly radiant, so blest
When sunset drapes the ardent west—
How more than beautiful art thou,
When the pure moon unveils her brow!
When star-rills trickle through the shade,
How more than radiant! How weighed
With all magnificence, all sweetness,
All power, all passion, all completeness.

It was a blissful, sacred hour,
That seemed most gloriously to flower
Out of deep evening, like the bloom
That draws its whiteness from a tomb.
A lustrous light-flood fell like rain;
A few light murmurs o'er the plain
Ran tenderly toward the ledge
That glistened at the river's edge,
And there, uniting with the cry
Of billows, floated to the sky.
It seemed that heaven itself had furled
The wing of peace around the world;
That the continuous music-surges,
Flowing from the extremest verges
Of the eternal sea of voice,
That calls unceasingly, "Rejoice!"
Had fallen toward creation's girth,
To touch the palsied lips of earth,
And woke a song therefrom as faint
As whisper of a dying saint.

Alas! that moons should glow and wax,
The murderer's straining sight to tax,
For glimpses of his victims' tracks!
That aught of beautiful should aid
Vindictive plan or vengeful raid.

And peaceful nature share the guilt,
When crimson, human blood is spilt!

Have ye not, in some dreamy hour,
That came, with moonlight-peace, to dower
Your slumb'rous senses, felt a power,
Wrathful and dark, speed swiftly in,
As 't were a marshaled host of sin;
And while, with sore amaze, you shook,
'Neath the wierd phantasm's glow'ring look,
You still have watched, by terror nerved,
The path, the awful presence curved,
Till all your soul's sweet light but served
The thousand hateful eyes to show,
That smote you with their baleful glow?
So, o'er the moon-illumined land,
Came a dark-browed and subtle band,
Whose very silence seemed to say,
How savagely they yearned for prey.
With stealthy tread, and tireless haste,
They swept through wood and barren waste,
Questioning, with evil eyes intent,
Of pebble moved, or grass-blade rent,
To learn which way the lovers went.
Slight were the marks;—a branch that hung
A little low; a twig down flung;

A late and faded flower that lay,
With half its petals torn away;
And these were all, until they stood
Close by a little tangled wood,
And marked, upon a moonlit mound,
Where many feet had trod the ground;
Tearing, as they assayed to pass,
The clinging, rush-leaved feather-grass,
That from one gay robe, fluttering through,
Had torn a bead, that shone like dew.

The night passed on her westward track,
And drew her radiant mantle back;
The moon grew dim, and hid her face;
Yet still Ne-pow-ra led the chase.
As if keen instinct could avail
To trace the faint, imperfect trail
Though all the light of heaven should fail.

Then the cool night laid down to rest,
With songless lip and shrouded breast,
And day across the heavens stole,
As shadowy as a poet's soul.
It came and passed, and came again,
Divided by a night of pain
That sobbed itself away in rain,

And seemed to fling its shadow gray,
Coldly o'er all the coming day.
That withered day! It seemed to lean
The frowning heaven and earth between,
As if some dreary tale of fear,
Had partly caught its sluggish ear;
And, gossip-like, to hear the rest,
It yearned with eagerness unblest;
But yearned in vain; its last, slow ray
Shrank from the weeping world away,
And left a ghastly light and dim,
Like that which marks a rainbow's rim,
When smothered in a cloud it lies,
And in a gradual tracery dies.

A pallid light, that like a robe
Of death, was folded round the globe;
But brightened with a star, and fringed
With swaying clouds, all whitely tinged
By the light-prophesying glow,
From the unrisen moon below.

Like a grieved child, the wind had wailed,
Until the fulvid daylight paled;
But when the twilight shade grew deep,

It slowly sobbed itself to sleep.
No murmur in the air; — no sound,
Was stealing o'er the dewy ground;
But, with a strange and ghastly grimness,
Dark forms were speeding through the dimness;
Each with as unresounding tread,
As step of spirit from the dead.

Beside the river's quiet breast,
The bridal train was hushed in rest;
The sky seemed tenderly to lean
Above them, and the clouds between
Drooped as they were a curtain screen;
And the slow stream crept deftly by,
Hushing its light song to a sigh,
Lest the light vail of twilight sleep
Should from each sealed eyelid sweep.

All suddenly a timorous cry
Arose, and pierced the silent sky: —
"Oconee! Wake! The foe is nigh!"
Instant as lightning at the sound
A score of warriors spurned the ground;
And, dashing down the silver dew,
Along the dark shore, westward flew.

Ne-pow-ra heard the voice; his eye
Saw the fleet braves before him fly;—
Amid the evening's gathering gloom
Caught one white gleam of tossing plume
And knew the glowing, scarlet vest,
That clung to Ulah's panting breast.
As the red meteor's streaming light
Makes the deep sable heavens bright,
So through his eyes' dark night there came
A sudden lightning burst of flame.

"Warriors!" he cried,"when wolves are nigh,
How the weak prairie-chickens fly!
Be strong as starving wolves, to tear
The feathered scalps these cowards wear!"

They heard;—as storm's red banner flies,
So leaped the lightning from their eyes;
And, like the thunder's awful blare,
A thousand war-whoops rent the air,
As if that soundless calm had been
A prophecy of future din;
And all the tempests of the world
In jangling unity were hurled,

To scare the skies with discord rude,
And waken hell to join the feud.

With lengthened leap, like panther's tread,
The sinewy forms, untiring, sped.
These, silent as the arrowy rays
That light the glittering polar ways;
Those, following with whoop and vaunt,
Mingled with curse and jeering taunt.
Fleet is the foot that terror flings;
But vengeance moves with fleeter wings.
Nearer, each waving crimson crest,
And nearer still, and nearer pressed.

Darkly, in the dim distance, towered
A massive rock, with cedars bowered;
Girt by the Illinois, that shone
At its dark feet, as, by a throne,
A cloth of shining silver lies,
And sparkles up to kingly eyes.
Most fit for kings, the boulder lay —
Majestic, strong, and stern as they —
The tyrant of the darkened land,
All isolated, cold and grand.
No foot could reach its lofty head,
Save by a narrow path that led,

Rock-guarded upward, rough and steep,
Impregnable as castle-keep.
Gray were its walls, but toned and vailed,
With clambering vines that o'er them trailed,
And glowing yet with blossoms rare,
That purpled in the summer air,
A hundred feet above the swarm
Of eddying waves it reared its form,
And gave the swooping raven rest
Upon its broad and mossy breast.
At its fringed side the heron stood,
With neck curved downward toward the flood,
Intent but on his silent prey,
Whose fins flashed through the river spray;
And there the broad-winged owl flew by,
All the long night, with hollow cry,
That seemed some harper's tuneless lay,
Prescient of dolor and dismay.

On sped the chase! The foe could hear
The pant of haste, the sigh of fear;
His bow each nimble warrior drew,
And aimed his arrow as he flew.

Beneath the rock's o'erhanging shade,

Where deepest glooms of night were laid,
The little band were screened; then, first,
A cry from the young chieftain burst:
"Ulah! my braves! in boyhood's day,
My feet have climbed this rocky way;
And oh! be glad once more, for thus
Has the Great Spirit cared for us!"
Then, linked with Ulah, led the flight
Up the dark bluff's gigantic hight,
And, searching o'er the broken side,
Found a safe covert for his bride.
One lingering look, a kiss, a word,
That moved the lips, and sunk unheard;
Then backward to the path he sprang,
And loud his bold defiance sang:

"Ye are a mighty band, and we
Are little, and we could but flee;
Yet follow here, and our swift darts
Shall fly, and tear your serpent hearts!"

Not death itself such hearts could daunt!
Yell answered yell, vaunt echoed vaunt;
From every rock-cleft crevice rang
The bursting war-whoop's deafening clang,
And horridly, from plains below,

Rose the mad screeching of the foe.
Hither and thither, at the base,
Circled the wild, uncertain chase,
Till, vainly searching for the path,
They could but pause in baffled wrath.

But, now, like one scared out of rest,
Who flings the curtains from her breast,
The moon struck back the clouds of night,
And leaned between them still and white.
By the wild gleaming of her face,
The narrow road each eye could trace;
And there, like wild beasts by their caves,
Stood the young chieftain and his braves.

Now burst anew that awful sound,
And trampling legions shook the ground;
Onward his band Ne-pow-ra led—
Downward the flint-tipped arrows sped;
And, like a meteoric rain,
The far-flung stones shot to the plain;
Till, close uniting at the base,
Face from above leaned down to face;
And, glowering with intensest light,
Made luminous the pallid night.

Dire, dire confusion! not a cry
Could, unattended, pierce the sky;
But shout, and groan, and dying yell,
Blended in one terrific swell,
Till e'en the startled eagle rose,
Screaming with terror o'er the foes.

Soon, soon the burst of opening battle
Changed for the smothered, deathful rattle
From gasping throats, and groans suppressed
Were stifled in the heaving breast.
Beside the river's flinty bed,
A hundred valiant braves lay dead;
And the fierce wolf stole o'er the plain,
With hungry haste to lap the rain
That dripped from many a gaping wound,
And, hot and crimson, warmed the ground.

Oh! twice ten thousand men would fail
That narrow, guarded road to scale.
Though but a score might fling their darts,
That score could pierce a score of hearts
With every lifted bow, and still
Creep from the enemy at will.

Like some strong beast withheld from prey,

Ne-pow-ra stood. The flaming ray
That leaped within his glaring eyes
Almost might make the dying rise.
Suddenly, toward the rocky path
He flew, like one on fire with wrath,
Cleft the dark ranks that paused beneath,
And, frenzied, rushed alone to death.

Oconee saw him in the gloom,
And knew him by his kingly plume:
Fleetly, toward his towering head,
Winged with a curse, the elf-bolt fled;
Met him, as up the hight he pressed,
And sunk into his maddened breast.

He paused; like some still forest tree,
He stood a space; then turned to flee;
But, ere his failing foot could leap,
Reeled, and swung, powerless, down the steep.
Prone at the rock's rough foot he lay,
And, dumb and senseless, barred the way.

Forth, at the sight, Pauwega sprang,
While the thick arrows round him sang;
And, with a giant strength, he bore
The chieftain from the rock-girt shore.

But now a deeper darkness clung,
And hid the pale moon where she swung;
And, softly gathering up the dead,
A little way the warriors fled ;
While, 'neath the fir-tree at the base,
The wakeful sentry took his place,
That no light feet should steal away,
And rob the savage of his prey.

Soon did the silence round them steal,
And set on every lip her seal ;
While sleep, from out night's cool dominion,
Sailed softly on with dusky pinion;
And hovering o'er the wildest sense,
Wrapped it in stirless impotence.

Sweet sleep, that comes to all alike —
The weak who sink, the strong who strike;
Soft as the moonlight's milky glow,
And gentle as a river's flow!
All day our weary ways we feel
Along the world, as blind men steal,
Uncertain where the foot will sink —
On flowery bed, or chasm's brink;
But, in the night, we gently take
The robe of Deity, to make

A tent for our tired souls, and dare
The darkness, certain of His care.
And, oh! when sorrow's tempests sweep,
How pleasant is the calm of sleep!
So like that faint, exhaling breath
That men have dared to christen Death!
Christened with tears on earth ; but when,
Lifting no more the breast of men,
Like a rose-perfumed, balmy gale,
It swells an ANGEL's heaven-bound sail.

CANTO V.

Ne-pow-ra lived — if life can flow
When its red tide has sunk so low.
With gathered grass they piled his bed,
Pillowed with moss his stirless head,
And laid him where his wakening eye
Could, unobstructed, sweep the sky.

All night in deathly trance he lay; —
Scarce could they feel life's fountain play
Within his breast, and on his face
A stern and awful look had place,
As if his hatred and despair,
Even in his rest, were printed there.
At earliest dawn, returning life
Made in his heart a little strife
With deathful languor, and a glow
Crept to his cheek in gradual flow,

As it had caught the crimson dyes
That tinted all the orient skies;
And, while reflecting, faintly grew,
Lit with a kindling morning too.

He moved a lid;—his first slow gaze
Seemed to dawn forth in shrouding haze;
But suddenly flashed full and high,
While from his lips a gasping cry
Came hoarsely, "Let the cowards die!"
He said no more; but what he said
Told of some purpose deep and dread;
And to the savage senses came,
His meaning, through his eye of flame.

There have been those, who, clear of guilt,
Have, in their dream, some sweet life spilt;
And, hardly out of sleep, have deemed
The horror done, that was but dreamed,
And for one moment felt the smart
Of murd'rous purpose, in the heart.
In that wild instant, friend or foe
Beside them had been stricken low;
And the red gush of human gore
Had stained the hand forevermore.

Was it not thus?—had he not kept
Unholy warfare while he slept;
And, as he wakened, Frenzy planned,
And gave to air that fell command?

To let the hand of Famine rest
In icy pressure on the breast;—
To let her thin arm's close embrace
Blacken the brightness of the face;—
To let her white mouth press the lip,
Till the last hissing breath should slip,
From quivering lungs, and Death should try
The heart-string's last wild minstrelsy;—
To let the fair, the living tread,
Above the caverns of the dead;
While, at the step, a hollow sound,
Rings from the straining, heaving ground;
To let the blooming hill of life
Grow pregnant, in a horrid strife,
And gape, until, within its womb,
The eye can trace a yawning tomb,
And the pale arms are linked among
The skeleton-arms around them flung;—
And the dread fissure, closing now,
Shuts in the breast, the lip, the brow;—
Oh, God! to let these horrors wind

Around the frenzy-shaken mind,
And stand, and watch the war, the while,
With a triumphant, fiendish smile;—
This was his deadly purpose:—Life,
With all delights and beauties rife,
And power, that lifts the spirit high
Between the valley and the sky;—
And love—a mightier thing—a sea
That sways the soul with ecstasy;—
All, all forever flung away,
For joy of one revengeful day.

Is *this* the *boasted human?* Can
Such hatred nerve the heart of man,—
Of *more* than man—of FATHER! Oh!
Let the skies into rivers flow!
Let the high suns dissolve in seas,
To wash such blood-soaked souls as these!

Yet these were savage! There have been
Darker and deadlier deeds of sin,
Among the "children of the light,"
That scoff at these dark sons of night;
A slander-sting, from one who grew,
In daylight, sweet as honey-dew;

And, big with word-love, at the heart
Aimed, secretly, his pois'nous dart;—
A father stabbed; a trusting wife,
Robbed of the bliss of mother-life;
A daughter ravished;—who can tell
Or number these? The brain would swell,
With anguish; the weak heart would quail;
The very springs of life would fail,
To hear them. Make the grave-rooms deep,
And let the awful terrors sleep.
But, oh! bow down! nor dare to say,
"*These* are of *night*, and *those* of *day:*"
None but the Holiest, Most Wise,
Can, in a conscious splendor rise,
And, leaning o'er sepulchral night,
Declare, "I DWELL IN PERFECT LIGHT."

———

The days moved drearily along—
A pallid and discordant throng.
The nights, with clouds of. terror crowned,
Dropped dews like death-damps to the ground.

Death was at work. The sluggish air
Was weighed with breathings of despair,

And humid with the briny rain,
That burst from every madd'ning brain;
But not a wailing cry arose,
To swell the joy of waiting foes;
'T was silent all;—you had not thought
That overhanging skies saw aught
But river broad and prairie green,
And the huge rock that lay between.
You had not deemed the chilly air
A sound upon its wings could bear,
Save the slow water's moaning hymn,
Blended with sigh of waving limb,
And broken into fragments rude,
By ravens' croaking interlude.

At length, along the world there came
An autumn day, half frost, half flame;
The red sun flung his banner high,
And fleet, cold winds went raving by.

Ne-pow-ra, rigid as the clay
From which the soul has fled away,
Lay on his couch;—his glassy eye
Turned hungrily toward the sky.
Hungering for what? For sound of grief,
From dying warrior or from chief;—

For sign of cowardice, or weak,
Shrill note of woman's plaintive shriek.

He would not die till he could know
The rarest vengeance of a foe;
Till he could say, "They cry for aid —
These women-warriors are afraid!"
Reddening with sudden vigor now,
Then cold and pale his swarthy brow,
As thoughts of deep revenge would start,
Or Death's dark anguish clutch his heart.

Ha! What has roused the leaping blaze
That flashes through his lifted gaze?
What nerves the dark'ning brain anew,
To light with life death's clinging dew?
What lifts him from his grassy bed,
And rears once more his haughty head?

See! On the boulder's mossy breast,
There gleams aloft a scarlet vest;
And through the air a sound of woe
Steals to the greedy ears below!

Could that be Ulah?—she whose face,

Had been the beauteous dwelling-place
Of bashful bloom, whose graceful ways
Had made fierce warriors chant her praise;
Whose swaying form was light and lithe;
Whose singing voice was sweet and blithe;
Whose glance was like the dusky night,
With all its sparkling stars alight.
Could *that* be *Ulah?* Bowed and weak,
With glaring eye and ashen cheek,
Swayed, like the wind-flower light and fair,
With every idle breath of air!
Alas! 'twas Ulah! Could he trace
The deathliness of that young face;
Or could he hear the anguished wail
That rose above the sounding gale;
Nor feel a power within his breast,
Rousing the dead love from its rest?
High on the beetling bluff she clung,
While the green cedars round her swung,
And leaned her ghastly face below,
Lit with her last hope's burning glow.
She saw him—knew him—and a prayer
Of yearning passion rent the air.

"Ne-pow-ra—father—oh! come nigh,
And hear thine erring daughter's cry;

Let the last flame of wrath depart,
And ULAH fill again thine heart.

"Oh! thou wert wont to say, her eye,
Like thine own glance, was brave and high;
And thou wert wont to say, her feet
Were, like her mother's, light and fleet!

"See! dim the eye that used to shine,
With lightning flame, as bright as thine;
And slowly now the feet must tread,
That go to join the mother, dead!

"Beneath the fir's dew-dripping bough,
The chieftain's daughter leans her brow;
While the tears, dripping from her eyes,
Freeze on the cold stone where she lies.

"Oh! thou wert wont, with willing feet,
To bring thy daughter tender meat;
And thou didst greet, with kindly word,
At morn and night thy singing bird!

"Thou knowest how Ulah oft did bring
For thee cool water from the spring;

And crush the maize, and build the fire,
To feed and warm her warrior sire.

"Ne-pow-ra—father—hear my cry!
Oh! give us food—we fail—we die!
Let the last flame of wrath depart,
And ULAH fill again thine heart!"

Vain prayer—to deaf, unheeding ear!
He heard not; or he would not hear.
As well might summer zephyrs hope
To tear the earth-bound boulder up;
Or glowing summer sun to fuse,
Or night dissolve the rock with dews,
As Ulah hope, with wail or prayer,
To ope the fount of mercy there;—
Revenge, or something mightier, drew
Forever from the rock its dew.

She passed away—the echo heard
No more the sound of pleading word;
Yet kept the air awhile astir,
In tender memory of her.

Unmoved the chieftain stood; nor bowed
His stately head; and if a crowd
Of memories swept his heart-strings, shaking

His purpose stern, or softly waking
The olden music there, no tone
Revealed the secret. God alone,
Whose ear at the deep heart is bent,
Knew what his awful stillness meant.

He stirred not—spoke not—silent awe
Lay like a spell on all who saw.
Oh! would he ever speak? The breeze
Harping its wierd, wild melodies,
Grew deathly still;—the very wave,
That seemed the pulse of nature, gave
No voice, but a low, throbbing sound,
That, like a heart-beat, shook the ground.

They broke the chain of that wierd spell;
They came; they touched him, and he fell;
They raised the plumed, and kingly head;
He stirred not, spoke not;—HE WAS DEAD.

If human deeds have power to draw
Aside inexorable law,
To dim the light of heaven, and tear

The sweetness from the ambient air;
To bow the heads of all bright things,
As if beneath dark, shadowing wings,
Then did the day receive the stain
Of deathful wound, and die in pain;
Upon the pallid, cloud-draped sky,
With ghastly heaviness, to lie,
Until the evening, white with fear,
Lifted her from her silent bier,
While all the mourning stars drew near,
And carried her, with tears like rain,
Down to the western burial-plain.
The sun's bright flame was quenched in mist;
The smothered winds grew calm and whist;
An icy chill crept o'er the land,
As if it felt Death's rigid hand
Shut round it, as in coffins cold,
A rose, the dead, white fingers fold;
A rose that withers in the deep,
Still night, that guards the grave's soft sleep;
A day that fades, like crimson roses,
In the black night that round it closes.

Just at the twilight, while a dirge
Came sweeping from the river surge,
A score of voices joined the swell,

In tardy clangor, like a bell
Struck solemnly and slowly first,
Then wakening to a rapid burst
Of sharp, successive peals, then dying,
Like a sick infant's last, soft sighing.
In quavering unity, they rose,
As they were one, until the close;
But shook apart, at the last stave,
Like a low, pebble-parted wave.
It was the death-song's loitering flow,
That startled even the ruthless foe,
With the wild grandeur of its woe,
Until it died, ere half descended,
In faint, and fainter murmurs ended.
The last low echo scarce was flown,
When the foe caught a clearer tone,
That, like a sudden trumpet-blast,
Full to the evening wind was cast.
Upon the boulder's topmost hight,
They saw, within the faded light,
Oconee, pallid as the dead,
Like a straight sapling, rear his head;
A parting cloud within the west
Let the last sunbeam kiss his breast;
While, with his arm toward heaven flung,
Thus his last song the warrior sung:

4*

"Let the gray wolf his watches keep;
He can not make Oconee weep;
Fierce hunger in his breast may rave;
His voice is strong, his heart is brave.

" Who says the chieftain fears to die?
Let the keen winds of night reply;
And with a loud, unfailing breath,
Repeat his happy song of death.

" He need not be ashamed; his bow
Has laid no weeping woman low;
No boy has trembled at his tread;
His hand has scalped no brother's head.

"Ere yet his early years had gone,
He learned to chase the flying fawn;
Scared the bold eagle from his nest,
And sent the arrow to his breast.

" The prairie-wolf, his voice to hear,
Crept to his hole and shook with fear;
And, if he sought the forest wide,
The screeching panther turned aside.

"Great Tautometa's bloody hand

Smote the weak tribes, and fired the land;
Oconee's fleet, unerring dart.
Drank the red river of his heart.

"Wi-com-i-ket was tall and brave
As trees that in the storm-wind wave;
With bursting yell, he scared the day;—
Oconee tore his scalp away.

"Now, while the night's great shadows fall,
Oconee hears his father call;
And sees the sunbeam in the west,
That waits to guide him to his rest.

"Who says the chieftain fears to die?
Let the loud winds fling back the lie!
And, stooping downward, tell the wave
How glad his heart is, and how brave."

Weak mockery of bravery! High
The trembling voice essayed to fly;
Swift but uncertain cleft the air,
And hung awhile suspended there;
Then dropped, like arrow-smitten bird,
And its last carol died unheard.

The starving moon that walked the sky,
With pallid face and patient eye,
Had pined away, with wasting charms,
And died in evening's circling arms;
When, to the boulder's towering head,
His braves the chief, Pauwega, led.
No more the fires of anger burned;
And even glutted vengeance turned
From his cold prey. No dripping blood
Had stained the rock with crimson flood;
But heavily each warrior-head
Was pillowed on its rocky bed;—
And never, in its loftiest hour,
Seemed crowned with more majestic power;
A power that struck each living heart
With icy fear, as with a dart;
And pressing back each sighing breath,
Triumphed o'er hatred, e'en in death.

Wrapped to her chieftain's faithful breast,
Did Ulah take her dreamless rest.
The dark, wind-shaken ivy trailed
Above her brow, so meekly vailed
With drooping tresses, and her face
Smiled on its swarthy resting-place,

Like a sweet flower of summer, lain
In autumn on the flame-scorched plain.

As streams, that to the giddy verge
Where rolls the cascade's beaten surge,
Their wild and willful courses urge,
Along their green banks gliding, single,
Till near the edge their torrents mingle,
Then, clasping closely loving palms,
Chanting, in death concordant psalms,
Leap down to linked and endless calms;—
So were these savage lovers. Deep
And peaceful their eternal sleep!
Who, such united fate could weep?

NOTES.

That I may stand in no danger of being thought guilty of literary piracy, I subjoin the following, which I found drifting away to oblivion, on the flood of newspaper literature; and which is the foundation of my little story.

I must, however, do myself the justice to say, that before meeting with this version of the legend, I had framed for myself the skeleton of a narrative quite similar to this, and in connection with the very rock which has, unquestionably, been the scene of some disastrous event. But thinking, perhaps, there was some degree of authenticity about the story already published, I at once abandoned my own plan, and proceeded to appropriate the work of some unknown individual; for which grand larceny, possibly, my readers would graciously pardon me, did they know my *own* explanation of the mystery of "Starved Rock."

It will be observed, that the story has undergone some alteration in my hands; but I hope I have not materially lessened its beauty. I have endeavored, very likely, with indifferent success, to " clothe the bare bough with sunny flowers;" and, for this purpose, have grafted in, here and there, a scion from my own stock.

But here you have the legend, as it first appeared, under the title of

"THE LEGEND OF THE STARVED ROCK.

" In the 'far West,' where broad, rolling prairies stretch away for miles in billowy undulations, towering up from the brink of a stream, rises a large boulder, called 'Starved Rock.'

"Its walls are of dark gray stone, half vailed with clambering wild-vines and trailing mosses — as some dilapidated castle, relic of feudal times, stands wrapped in the drapery which long ages have woven around it; and broken parapets, of stinted cedars and firs, frown threateningly at the daring adventurer who attempts to scale its precipitous steeps. A narrow, almost perpendicular path, on the side opposite from the river, is revealed as you make a circuit of the base of the cliff, and he who would reach the highest elevation of the rock can ascend.

"There is a fugitive tale commemorating the events which gave this wild cliff so singular a name. Long years ago, the brave and noble Indian chief, Oconee, leader of a powerful tribe, inhabiting the surrounding regions, saw and loved the gentle Ulah, daughter of his powerful rival, the chieftain of a neighboring tribe.

"Oconee was young and brave; and no warrior in the chase could bring down the fleet deer, or the fierce prairie-wolf, so sure as he.

"Ulah was young and fair, with eyes like the evening star, and dusky locks, like the gathering shades of night. She loved the brave Oconee; and, when he told her that his wigwam was spread with softest furs, and would she consent to share it, for her he would chase the deer and bring the young eaglet to her feet; then, in the midnight, she crept away from her father's lodge, and stole away with the young chieftain.

"Ne-pow-ra missed his daughter from his wigwam. When he came at evening from the toils of the hunt, she sprang not forth to meet him; when he came from the war-path or deadly ambuscade, exulting in victory, she went not forth with his braves, singing the war-songs of her race.

"The daughter of a chieftain was in the wigwam of his deadly foe. He could not brook the insult; and gathering his bold, fleet warriors about him at the council-fire, he recounted the wrong he had suffered, and bade them follow him to avenge it.

"Day after day, night after night, saw them on the trail of the pursued, guided by the starry heavens overhead, and the forest wilds beneath. Westward the stars of night guided their footsteps.

"On the fourth day, the eagle gaze of the fugitives saw the waving plumes of their pursuers in the distance. Before the young chieftain, bold and high rose the huge rock, on the brink of the Illinois; behind came the enraged Ne-pow-ra, with the fierce warriors of his tribe, the wind floating their wild cries of vengeance, and dancing ever nearer and nearer their eagle plumes.

"The pursued Oconee, with his dusky maiden, and a small band of his faithful braves, fled to the rocky fortress — the tower of strength — that rose precipitously in their path.

"On, on came the pursuers, with wild shouts and unearthly yells; on, on until they, too, reached the base of the cliff, and then shouting a loud war-cry, they rushed swiftly up the narrow pathway, resolved to meet the enemy on the summit. But the young chieftain's arm was strong; his arrows swift and sharp, and his braves resolved to fight until the death; so, one after another, as the warriors below sought to ascend the cliff, they were pierced by the unerring arrows from above, till they fell back, bleeding and wounded, amid their companions.

"Then, failing in this attempt, with half their band lying dead around them, the survivors closed in dark ranks about the base of the rock, under cover of the firs, with sullen silence, and invincible determination, to await the slow, lingering, horrible death of their victims, in the gloomy, desolate fortress above.

"Day after day, the red sun rose in the orient, wheeled across the burning heavens slowly toward the western horizon; but, to those on the high, huge boulder of gray stone, no relief came.

"Still, day by day, the withering sunbeams fell upon them, drying up their very life-blood; still, night by night, those gigantic shadows crept closer, shrouding their hearts. *They were starving.*

"And there, too, at the base of the cliff, silent and dusky, as the firs which shrouded them from the fierce sun-ray, sat that implacable chieftain, surrounded by his warriors. Neither love, mercy, nor pity entered his heart. His bitterest foe had stolen his fairest flower; vengeance on them both — the bitter foe, the faithless daughter!

Strong warriors who had not quailed in the deadliest combat, now sank down, like reeds before the breath of famine. With plenty beneath them, they were starving! Oh, it was horrible!

"And then the Indian maiden came to the brink of the precipice; and, with her long, dark hair streaming, like the folds of a rent banner on the air, bent down and pleaded with agonized gestures and frantic entreaties to her sire, whom she saw, far, far below. But never a tone of tenderness, or a token of reconciliation, went up from that insulted soul. He had chosen the *Indian's revenge!*

"Day by day, that doomed band thinned away, until at length Famine, alone, remained conqueror, on the summit of the cliff. No ghostly forms wandered about; no wailing woman's voice broke the silence.

"When all was silent upon the summit, the avenged chieftain and his band ascended.

"The Indian's wrath was appeased; his vengeance had, indeed, been terrible. There they lay upon the gray rock, those skeleton-like forms, all stark and stiff; and there, too, the gentle Indian maiden, Ulah, had died in the arms of her lover;— her ghastly face still bearing the impress of woman's devotion in her death hour; her long, streaming hair at once her bridal vail and shroud.

"And now, it is said, full oft, by the pale, shimmering moonlight, are seen, wan, ghostly figures, gliding to and fro upon the cliff, with dark plumes floating upon the night wind; and ever and anon the spectral forms of the Indian maiden and her dusky warrior-lover stand hand in hand upon the brink, and, in low, wailing voices, chant their death dirge, ere they go afar through the gate of Famine, to dwell together in the Great Spirit's happy hunting-grounds. Thus runs the Legend of Starved Rock."

And, lo! as we husked them, the red ears were mine!

It is a superstition among the Indian maidens that whoever finds a red ear, while plucking the corn, is sure of a husband.

ᵇ The Des Plaines river, after its union with the Fox, becomes the Illinois. Although the western rivers are almost invariably fringed with forest, yet, the "oldest inhabitant" of the region of country here described will tell you that time was when this stream ran through an unwooded land, where the eye could sweep for miles, seeing only now and then a grove.

ᶜ An incident similar to this, I am told, happened during a war between the Indians and Whites in that vicinity. A spy concealed himself amid the dense branches of the burr-oak, and was, thereby, enabled to report accurately, among the Whites, the movements of the enemy.

ᵈ The prairie-wolf lives in holes, burrowed in the open plain, of from ten to thirty feet in depth.

THE REIGN OF TRUTH.

Ho, ye sluggish nations of earth!
   The dark bird, Night, from her haunt has risen:
And through the land a sound of mirth
   Welcomes the sun from his orient prison.
Awake! for the fair, broad light of truth
Is bringing this old world back to youth.

Long has it lain in Tyranny's arms,
   Compassed about with doubt and terror;
Wrathfully tossed in mighty storms,
   Borne on the tides of wrong and error;
Yet shall nothing the ship o'erwhelm —
Truth, like a pilot, takes the helm.

Sorrow haunteth earth's lowly homes;
   Frenzy aboundeth, and superstition;
Vice, at the gates of princely domes,
   Enters and pleads her deadly mission.

Lo! where Virtue, and Peace, and Ruth,
Walk by the side of queenly Truth.

Up, ye slumbering ones, awake!
    On to your labor, strong and hearty!
Work for the Truth — for the Truth's dear sake,
    Not at the call of sect or party.
On to the struggle, sons of earth!
Show your manliness; prove your worth.

Mammon hath sold the poor their bread,
    Taking their strength and life in payment;
Pride hath lifted her mocking head,
    Vain of the price of her rainbow raiment.
Scorn them all with their hateful arts;
Scourge them out of your homes and hearts.

Oh, ye lovers of Truth, arouse!
    What care ye for the world's opinion?
See where cringing Policy bows;
    Have ye a mind to be his minion;
On, at the cost of lash or stake!
    Work for the Truth — for the Truth's dear sake!

THE REIGN OF TRUTH.

All humanity cries aloud,
   Cowering under a dark existence;
Traveling on through mist and cloud,
   Nowhere seeing a happy distance.
Oh! if ye long for bliss and ruth,
Welcome the coming of queenly Truth.

Over the turbulent sea she rides,
   Down from the realms of light descended;
Smiling, she governs the roaring tides;
   "Peace!" At her word the storm is ended.
Shout! for the golden reign of Truth
Is bringing this old world back to youth.

On to the future's radiant shore!
   Soon shall hatred to love be turning;
Vice and error shall be no more;
   Doubt shall flee from the halls of learning.
See where the dark bird, Night, departs!
Peace shall enter your homes and hearts.

HIDE AND SEEK.

Down by the garden paths, winding,
    Fearing to laugh or to speak,
They hid; and Kate, who was "blinding,"
    Came from her goal to seek.

Under the flowering currant,
    The meddlesome breezes blew,
And carried Susie's white garment
    Out into Katie's view.

Away, with musical laughter,
    Over each bed and knoll,
Katie, with Susie after,
    Hurried to touch the goal.

Then, by the honeysuckle
    And red rose clusters gay,
With many a gleeful chuckle,
    Both of them looked for Mae.

They peered, with dubious glances,
   Where the bright lily-worts grew,
Lifting their leaves, like lances,
   Out of the morning dew.

In all its pretty regalia,
   Each garden posie smiled;
But daffodil, nor dahlia,
   Covered the hidden child.

Then they talked 'neath the lilac cover,
   And said, "Where can she be?
We have hunted the garden over,
   But nothing of Mae can see."

Then a voice, with a light sweet chuckle,
   Of triumph and glee combined,
Rang out from the honeysuckle,
   "I guess it's because you're so blind."

The weeks went by; the summer
   Lay down, with her flowers, to die;
The red leaves dropped upon her,
   And clouds came into the sky.

And down at the garden ending,
  Mournfully gazing around,
Two little girls were bending
  Over a newly-made mound.

Under the dark atropa,
  Carefully hidden away,
Slept the white-garmented baby—
  The delicate, beautiful Mae.

With grief in their sweet eyes lying,
  Tenderly, hand in hand,
Questioning and replying,
  Did the innocent maidens stand.

"Mamma says, the dear angels love us,
  And come to us every day;
May be, just now, they're above us,
  And, with them, our sister Mae."

"Then why can't we see her, Katie?
  Let's look for her, up in the skies."
And upward, with tear-drops weighty,
  She lifted her azure eyes.

Their rivaling blue swept the ether,
    But nothing of Mae could find;
She whispered, "I can not quite see her;
    I guess it's because I'm so blind."

———

Sweet children, the mists of the morning
    Only dim the white clouds in the blue;
Even so are the fair wings of angels
    But partially hidden from you.

Borne into our arms by the ocean
    Of life-waves that surge o'er the world,
Ye are swayed with continual motion,
    As if your own wings were unfurled.

But our eyes are heavy with sorrow;
    We wave our weak wings never more;
Your hope and your faith we must borrow,
    Before to your knowledge we soar.

PEACE.

There fell upon my soul a shadow dreary;
   'T was the heart's evening following the day;
With its long thought my toiling brain was weary,
   And scarce could frame the prayer my lips would say.

In the soul's oratorio, kneeling lowly,
   Thus with the Giver of my life I plead:
"Oh, let the seraph, Peace, high-browed and holy,
   Bind her white flowers around my aching head.

All my sad soul dissolved in that petition;
   Then to my prayer, a "still, small voice" replied,
"Peace, of love's labor is the glad fruition—
   The heritage that waits the furnace-tried."

Then answer made I none — my heart was
    shaken;
As the spent dove clasped by the hungry
    hawk,
So was my soul by gray-winged dread o'ertaken,
    And felt strange doubts its mighty yearnings
    mock.

Then said I to my soul, "Where is thy labor?
    And where the cure thy healing touch hath
    wrought?
Hast thou sought out thy sorrowing friend or
    neighbor,
    And fed him with the bread of holy thought?

"Hast thou not loved thyself, oh, mournful
    spirit!
More than all living things on land or sea?
Thou hast! Then, thine own bitter thoughts
    inherit;
    For the white flowers of Peace are not for thee.
"Never for thee, until thy selfish grieving
    Dies in warm sympathy for others' woe;
Then shall sweet Peace, unholy darkness cleav-
    ing,
    High-browed and radiant, beside thee go."

LOCUST LEAVES.*

I listened all the day,
   To the faint leaf-songs I heard,
Till each light roundelay
   Thrilled to my heart like a word.

Each like a low, sweet word,
   And out of the words there grew
A tale, but faintly heard;
   Yet I knew in my heart 't was true.

'T was true; for the locust leaves,
   That gayly and airily waltz
From the window up to the eaves,
   Would tell to me nothing false.

"Dost know, dear girl," they said,
   "That an old and mystic spell

*The green leaves of the locust tree are symbolical of a buried heart.

Is woven about the head
  Of the tree thou lovest well?

"It was once, in the ages gone,
  When the sun and the stars were blind,
And the moon went groping on
  For the light she could not find.

"Or ever the world knew day,
  Or ever an eye could see,
That a germ in the dark earth lay;
  'Twas the heart of the locust tree.

"'Twas the heart of the locust tree,
  In silence awaiting there
The touch of the sunlight free,
  And the breath of the morning air.

"Then a shaft of warm, new light
  Gleamed over the earth's dark way;
'Twas a sweet farewell to night;
  'Twas the ushering in of day.

"And, lo! the mountains bowed,
  And the deepening oceans grew;

And forth the winged cloud
　　Went laden with precious dew.

"The trees, like stately kings,
　　Uprose in the balmy air;
And their branches waved like wings;
　　But the locust stood not there.

"Low down in darkness slept
　　The little, lifeless germ;
And the ivy o'er it crept
　　With the serpent and the worm.

"The sunlight, on its bed,
　　Could never a thrill impart;
And the wind went by, and said,
　　''T is the tree of the buried heart.'

"It chanced that an angel heard,
　　'Mid melodies, light and free,
The sound of that pitying word,
　　And flew to the buried tree.

"She parted the ivy vine,
　　She loosened the earth around;

And the rich and warm sunshine
   Crept into the clay-cold ground.

"She smiled, and afar there drew
   The serpent and crawling worm;
She wept, and the holy dew
   Went down to the slumbering germ.

"'Come forth!' the angel said;
   'Lo! all things wait for thee;'
And out of its lowly bed
   Uprose the locust tree.

"Broadly its branches grew,
   With sprays all slender and light;
And flowers that had caught the hue
   Of the angel's robe of white.

"And, lo! in the twilight pale,
   Close under the drooping eaves,
Thou hearest the pleasant tale
   Of its airily-waltzing leaves."

But the last faint gleam of day
   Stole over the western hill;

The low breeze died away,
    And the locust leaves were still.

And I, at my window-pane,
    Did wonderingly repeat
To my heart, again and again,
    Their words so low and sweet.

"And there's many a heart," I said,
    "That needs but an angel's care,
To rise from its shrouding bed
    And wake from its deep despair.

"And the poisonous things above
    The slumbering heart of youth
Would flee at the smile of love,
    And fade in the light of truth."

GLEN ELGIN.

Sometimes, when my lip has forgotten its mirth,
When the pain in my heart makes me weary of earth,
When my cheek has grown wet with the fast-falling tears,
I love to remember my earliest years.

Glen Elgin, my home! I remember it well,
Where, bright in its beauty, the cataract fell;
Where the sun-painted bow sweetly smiled on the spray,
And the crane and the king-fisher watched for their prey.

I remember the bower that the long branches made
O'er the brake and the dwarf-yew that grew in the shade,
Where the robin trilled sweetly his beautiful song,

And the creek, with low laughter, went rippling along.

Where I laved my bare feet in its clear running tide,
And sprang o'er the wild, rugged rocks by its side;
And climbed through the rough tangled thicket, to search
For the tart sumac-drupe and the fragrant black birch.

I remember the place where so often I stood,
'Neath the cedar-crowned rock, in the depth of the wood,
Where the Solomon's seal decked the green, mossy bed,
And the jack-in-the-pulpit was nodding his head.

I used to lie down by the shadowy spring,
To hear the shy locust his monody sing;
For I fancied, (such thoughts through the young brain will reel,)
'T was a dear fairy grandmother spinning her wheel.

GLEN ELGIN.

I remember the course of the bright-leaping rill,
As it stole from the spring down the side of the hill,
Where the light was so dim all the long summer day,
And the jewel-weed blossomed, impatient and gay.

'Tis years since I wandered, a light-hearted child,
Through the depth of that valley, so tangled and wild;
Since I gathered the pale, purple flowers of the glade,
And bounded in glee by the foaming cascade.

I am wiser, perhaps, yet so little of woe
Did my soul in its freshness and purity know,
That I love to remember, wherever I roam,
The lovely Glen Elgin, my happiest home.

REMINISCENCES.

WRITTEN AT GLEN ELGIN, 1856.

Ah! once again the well-known road,
    With eager feet, I tread;
And memories come thronging back,
    Of days that long since fled,
When merry forms were here, that now
    Lie low among the dead.

On either side, the tall pines bend,
    To greet me as I go;
And voices, with their murmurs, blend
    In welcome, soft and low.
They seem to me like dear old friends,
    That loved me long ago.

And hark! the sound of singing birds!
    The birds I used to hear,
Are caroling their sweetest songs

To greet the wanderer's ear.
Old and familiar tunes are they
　To my young childhood dear.

A sound of laughter pealeth out—
　A ringing shout of glee;
And little, active forms, beside
　Our school-room door, I see;
And lo! the very spot where stood
　Our bench, beside the tree.

Around these deep, secluded woods,
　How many memories cling!
Just yonder is the bending bough,
　Whereon we used to swing;
And here's the very log where we
　Our noontide meal would bring.

And here, along this beaten path,
　We ran, with childish grace,
And dipped our heated feet within
　The swiftly running "race;"
Then bent above the wave, and laughed
　At each distorted face.

And here's the deep, romantic glen—
  The spot most loved of all,
Where brightly, in the spring-time, gleams
  The swollen waterfall,
Where, like sweet little ones at play,
  The answering echoes call.

Among these broken, moss-grown rocks,
  I've dreamed my childish dreams;
And plucked the purple flowers that grew
  Within their ragged seams;
And listened to the tiny shouts
  Of little falling streams;

And mocked the gleeful songs of birds
  That soared above my head;
And o'er and o'er my little rhymes,
  In musing mood have said,
Till I could almost think the rocks
  Have learned to know my tread.

I call aloud, and answering words,
  From rock and hill-side ring;
Ah! these are friends that will not mock
  The simple songs I sing;
And, while I have one memory left,
  My heart shall round them cling.

A CHICK-A-DEE SONG.

"Chick-a-dee dee dee dee dee!"
Now, what have you come to see,
With your scholarly "thinking cap" that lies,
Black as a coal, above your eyes,
Like a college president's comical crown,
When he sits in stiff commencement-gown,
And blinks as knowingly as though
He had fathomed all deep streams below?
Ah! you are as wise as he,
Chick-a-dee dee dee dee dee.

"Chick-a-dee! chick-a-dee dee dee!"
Well, what do you think of me,
Little philosopher? Here I lie,
Quietly, under your studious eye,
While you peer, and ponder, and noisily shout,
Can not you ferret the mystery out?
Saw you ever so queer a thing
Out of the green earth blossoming?

Is it plant, or shrub, or tree,
Chick-a-dee, chick-a-dee dee dee?

"Chick-a-dee dee dee dee dee!"
How dare you make so free!
Pulling so petulantly at my dress,
What is it, pretty one? can not you guess?
Then you must do as learned gentlemen do;
And batter the wall you may never get thro',
With so many bomb-shells of ponderous words,
That you quite bewilder the ignorant birds,
   Who are listening to you and me,
   And they cry, "Chick-a-dee, D. D."

"Chick-a-dee! chick-a-dee dee dee!"
What a musical burst of glee!
Very improper. Hav n't you heard,
Curious, little, pedantic bird,
Certain chick-a-dee gossips say,
Parsons shouldn't be light and gay?
And, clad in your sober, clerical coat,
With a white cravat around your throat,
   Do you know you are preaching to me,
   Chick-a-dee! chick-a-dee dee dee?

"Chick-a-dee dee dee dee dee!"
How many a thing we see,
And babble about, with busy tongue,
That puzzles the old as well as the young!
And who with flutter and noisy shout,
Could ferret every mystery out;
And weigh, in the delicate scale of mind,
Each new and wonderful thing we find!
Such little philosophers we,
Chick-a-dee! chick-a-dee dee dee!

A SONG FOR REFORMERS.

Sweep on, ye bright souls, unaffrighted and strong;
Sweep on, ye were born to annihilate wrong.
By the broad sea of Progress break down the high piers,
Where the bigot would anchor futurity's years.

Sweep on, o'er the mountains, where legions have striven,
In vain, for a glimpse of the cloud-curtained Heaven!
Where they trembled to hear the death-avalanche leap;
And like pebbles, insensate, were hurled down the steep!

Down, down, through the valleys descend, till ye bear
Your sun-lighted ensign through realms of despair;

While, like happy voiced birds, all the children
    of clay
Shall be startled to song in the glory of day.

Dark, dark, are the phantoms ye'll meet in your
    path;
And wild beasts are prowling, on missions of
    scath;
'Mid the blackness of ignorance, sulphurous fire
Streams over the dark-wreathing smoke of de-
    sire.

Lo! this dumb ossuary, the world, slumbers still!
Clothe anew these bare bones, by the might of
    your will;
Let the flames of your passion, all sacred and
    warm,
Leap, electric and glad, through each death-
    smitten form.

Behold! o'er society's storm-shaken sea,
The tyrant, aloft, like an osprey, rides free;
Sail down, like the bald eagle, tameless and
    brave,
The prey from his ravishing talons to save.

Yet, be not the eagle that robs to devour;—
Let mercy's bow smile o'er the storms of your
    power;
While the bird seeks his nest in security still;—
For ONE sees the wrong—let HIM smite, if he
    will.

Let your warcry arise o'er the king-ridden
    ground,
Till the dull ear of earthliness thrills at the
    sound.
Smite the riveted fetters that bind down the
    slave,
Till he leaps, in his joy, like a wind-smitten
    wave.

On, on, bright reformers! the voice of your
    prayer,
O'er your altars of sacrifice, cleaves the dense
    air;
The Holy One hears, and his answering fires
Fall earthward, to hallow your funeral pyres.

Your efforts are holy; your faces all shine
With the glow ye have caught from the ruler
    divine.

Ye have stood on the mountain, conversing
with Jove;—
Come down and illumine the vales with your
love.

Ye go not unguarded; for where ye have gone,
The sun-bright battallions of glory are drawn;
And, over your ways, an omnipotent arm,
By the strength of its sacredness, keeps you
from harm.

Sweep on! when your heavenly desirings are
crowned,
How brightly will blossom this blood-reeking
ground;
And, the earth, like a soul, from its sick body
riven,
Shall bathe in the soft healing rivers of Heaven.

THE SILVER CHALICE.

The morn did her sweet face uplift.
Beneath her, gathering mists did drift,
And falling rains were cool and swift.

The flowers, by holy love impelled,
Drew near to where the brooklets welled,
And with their waves sweet converse held.

And brooks and flowers smiled again,
And sang in love the low refrain,
"How sweet, how gentle is the rain."

A maiden, in the early day,
Came gliding o'er the flowery way,
And in her hand a chalice lay.

A silver chalice, frail and light,
As lily's lifted cup of white,
Or tiny sea-shell vases bright.

'Twas wrought with rare and wondrous art,
Like curling rose leaves, just apart;
Smile not — it was the maiden's heart.

The lilies bent with bashful grace,
As by their side the maid did place,
With tender care, her silver vase.

How sweetly shone her eye of blue,
Where eager hopes were shining through;
"Gather," she said, "Love's holy dew."

The light came down, subdued and dim;
The rain-drops sang their morning hymn;
The vase was laden to the brim.

The maiden's hand reached forth to take
Her chalice, when, by flower and brake,
Before her, came a gliding snake.

'Twas rare to see his crest of red,
As lightly to the maid he sped,
With quivering form and lifted head.

'Twas rare to see each rainbow scale,

That clad him like a coat of mail,
Changing beneath the daylight pale.

And, "If thou com'st," the maiden cried,
"To share my draught, thou'rt not denied."
The serpent glided to her side.

He looked into her laughing face,
Then twined around her silver vase,
And crushed it in his dread embrace.

Ah! had the maiden learned to know
That pride is Love's most bitter foe,
She had not felt that crushing woe;

But, with the flower and rippling rill,
Had quaffed Love's precious draught at will,
And borne her silver chalice still.

CHARITY.

Now, what bad thing is this
   That cowers beside the spring?
Surely, the hand hath wrought amiss
   That made so dull a thing.
I shudder to see it, and shrink
Away to the furthest brink;
For its black eyes stare and blink,
   With a look of reptile guile;
And I can but sicken, and think
   It is loathsome and vile.

   Strange that evil and gloom
      Are thrust in every place!
I can not pluck a summer bloom,
      But a worm is on its face;
And close by the song-bird, bliss,
Like a frown that follows a kiss,
Such venomous things as this
   Finish the tenderest strain,

With a hateful croak, or hiss,
    And a sound of pain.

"Look!" said a gentle one,
"It lies in a shady lair;
I draw it under the smiling sun;
    And, lo! it is good and fair.
It has colors of green and gold,
In many a changeable fold,
And in its delicate feet are soled
    With a web, like a tissue of Lisle.
See how it brightens the mold!
    Is it loathesome and vile!

"So, let but charity's light,
    Shine on the faultiest thing,
And, straightway, it glistens in raiment bright,
    As if it were blossoming.
Behold! it is not alone,
By the outward look and tone,
That the inmost soul is known;
    For a loving heart may smile,
When a darkened, loveless face is shown,
    And we cry, "*It is vile.*"

WAITING.

Down in the hollow, how cool and still!
The light crosses o'er from hill to hill;
And the wind has forgotten to wing so low,
Basking above in the sun's soft glow.
  Low in the hollow,
  The calm, deep hollow,
I wait alone — alone, in my woe.

Down in the hollow stands never a tree,
To bend with a whisper of love o'er me;
But the bath-flower patiently leans her head,
With plenteous tears, on the moss-grown bed.
  Low in the hollow,
  The calm, still hollow,
I wait, with a tearless, voiceless dread.

Down in the hollow, the maidenhair
Stands unrocked in the stirless air,
Where the silently-flowing, sluggish wave
Hides away 'neath the green bank's closing cave.

WAITING.

      . Low in the hollow,
        The calm, cold hollow,
How drear to be waiting the gloom of the grave!

High on the hillside—how calm and bright,
Is the fall of the beautiful, silvery light!
And the wind sings a psalm, like a spirit blest,
With the passion of worship warming its breast.
        High on the hillside,
        The glad, bright hillside,
I wait for a glimpse of my mansion of rest.

High on the hillside, the juniper tree
Leans with a whisper of love o'er me,
And visitor birds, with their heaven taught lays,
Rouse my glad spirit to rapture and praise.
        High on the hillside,
        The echoing hillside,
My voice in a pean of joy I raise.

High on the hillside, the shadow flies,
Frightened away by the beautiful eyes,
That look at me o'er the heavenly gate
With a yearning compassion that banishes hate.
        High on the hillside,
        The love-bright hillside,
How sweet for the transfiguration to wait!

THE KING OF THE NORTH.

The winter, the mirth chilling winter hath passed
From our home, on his icy track, away;
And hushed is the shout of the whirling blast,
And the sound of his wild and solemn lay.

He has gone to the north, the brave old north,
Where glimmer his crystal palace-halls;
Where never is heard the song of bird,
Or the sound of rushing water falls.

Where stars are bright in the pallid night,
He stalks alone, like a sentry old;
He smileth not—he weepeth not;
For his brow and his heart are icy cold.

But the glance of his eye is wild and high;
And the sound of his voice is clear and strong;

And the forests sigh, as he hurries by,
For he carols a bold and terrible song.

"I sweep o'er the earth, bringing wailing and dearth;
And my sounding wings are broad and fleet;
Woe! woe to the flowers, of the warm summer-hours,
I crush them all with my snow-white feet.

The clouds that lie in the far blue sky,
If I but pass with my chilling breath,
Rush down to their rest on the world's cold breast,
As white as the brow of the angel Death.

And the coward, man, grows pallid and wan;
And he shrinks away from my bold embrace.
I laugh at his plaint, when his heart grows faint,
And I mock him in his dwelling-place.

But I love to stand in the brave north-land,
Where glimmer my crystal palace-halls;
Where never is heard the song of bird,
Or the sound of rushing water falls.

And there, in the gleam of the star-light beam,
I stalk, like a sentry, grim and old;
And I sing at the sight of the northern light;
But my brow and my heart are icy cold."

THE CHILD—THE MAIDEN—THE MOTHER.

When the world-awakening sunlight
   Gushed through morning's gates of pearl,
From the realm of mystic shadow
   Came there forth a little girl.

Wandering by the winding streamlets,
   'Neath the young day's loving smile,
Gathering blue and golden violets,
   Full of little thoughts the while;

Thus the poet-child sped fleetly,
   Twining daises in her hair,
Wondering, as she caroled sweetly,
   Who had made the world so fair.

Wondering what the sun was doing,
   That he grew so bright and warm;

Wondering if he looked beneath him,
And espied her tiny form.

Half believing that the cloudlets,
Floating brightly robed above,
Were the forms of angel children —
White winged messengers of love.

Calling to them as they passed her,
"Little sisters, hasten here;
Here are violets and daisies,
And the brook is laughing near.

"I will give you all my flowers,
Laden, as they are with dew;
And the birds are singing softly;
Come, and they will sing for you.

"Come to me!" and Echo answered,
"Oh, sweet sister, come to me!"
Thinking 'twas an angel calling,
Laughed she then in quiet glee.

Murmuring with the murmuring zephyrs,
Singing with the singing birds,

Hearing every thing around her
  Utter low and loving words.

Thus the poet child sped lightly,
  Like a dream across the plain,
With her blue eyes beaming brightly,
  Caroling her simple strain.

In a dim and quiet forest,
  Where the summer breezes strayed,
With a low, melodious rustle,
  Walked, at noon, the poet-maid.

Many tender, mournful fancies,
  Busy at her heart alway,
As she stole along the pathway,
  Where the softened shadows lay.

Through the branches dropped the sunlight,
  Like a crown upon her hair;
And a thousand rippling noises,
  Melted in the balmy air.

Earnest thought her young brow shadowed,
  Tears were falling from her eyes;

Murmuring sadly, while the breezes
  Uttered low and sweet replies.

"Oh, the air is weighed with music!
  As I glide these aisles along,
Every living thing around me
  Sendeth up a joyful song.

"And its tiny bells uplifting,
  In the green and mellow light,
Blooms the lily of the valley,
  Clad in vesture snowy white.

"Flickering sunlight flames around me;
  Words mysterious thrill my ear;
Fancy's golden chain hath bound me;
  Even love might loiter here.

"Beauteous, quiet, loving nature!
  Like a harp thy rich voice sings,
When thy great, all-wise Creator
  Lays his hand upon the strings.

"Oh! there is a harp that slumbers
  In the heart, in silence deep,

Breathing only its sweet numbers
   When Love's fingers o'er it sweep.

"Meek-eyed lily of the valley,
   Stainless as an angel's thought,
Thou art flowering larger, whiter,
   By the holy sunbeam taught.

"Bird, that swings within the tree-top,
   In a deftly woven nest,
'T is the sunlight brings the song-tide,
   Gayly pulsing from thy breast.

"And, 'mid all the wondrous music
   Of this dim and voiceful grove,
Thus my darkened spirit yearneth
   For the blessed light of love.

" As the sunlight to the lily,
   As the perfume to the breeze,
As the young bird to the summer,
   As the green leaves to the trees,

"As the starlight to the evening,
   As the music to the grove,

As the dewfall to the flower,
  So to my young heart is love."

Sadly thus the poet-maiden
  Sang her low, unquiet tune,
While around her, perfume-laden,
  Stole the balmy breath of June.

———

On a steep and rugged mountain,
  'Neath the fading eye of day,
Walked a sad, sick-hearted mother,
  O'er a dark and toilsome way.

Autumn winds, around her sighing,
  Uttered many a mournful wail;
In the west the sun was dying,
  And the light was cold and pale.

Dews upon her head were falling;
  Chill and damp the evening air;
And the mother, faint and weary,
  Lifted up the voice of prayer.

"Holy father, guard my loved ones,"
  Thus the weeping mother cried;
"Many snares are spread around them;
  Thou, alone, canst safely guide.

"From thy Being's boundless ocean,
  Thou didst draw them with thy smile;
Keep these dew-drops of the human
  From the courses that defile.

"As the breaking cloud of evening
  Flings its rain upon the sea,
So, ETERNAL WAVE of fullness,
  Do I leave my pearls with thee."

Earnest, loving-hearted mother,
  Voices call thee from afar;
Lo! above thy darkened pathway,
  Beameth evening's golden star.

Lo! the child hath heard an angel;
  Love hath cheered the maiden's breast;
And the weary, suffering mother
  Entereth an eternal rest.

THE TIDE OF LIFE.

Oh, silent and mysterious tide!
Where'er thy gentle waters glide,
Sweet living things awake and move,
Responsive to thine earnest love.

Along the world's continuous round,
How do thy surging waves abound!
Throbbing, with sway supremely mild,
In bird, in rosebud, or in child.

Nature, thine handmaid, guides the way,
Across the bare, unfruitful clay;
And the dumb seed, unthrilled before,
Opes wide for thee her darkened door.

Thou enterest in;— from earth's cold breast,
Transformed she springs, in beauty dressed;
Glad in existence just begun,
Shakes her green garments in the sun.

From the brown mold the lilies rise,
Slow to unveil their dreamy eyes,
Like maiden, on her marriage-day,
Bending, with folded hands, to pray.

The rustling reeds rock to and fro
With gentle sound, sedate and slow,
Like mother, when the day is dim,
Chanting a love-born cradle-hymn.

Oh, wondrous tide of life! Thy power
Paints cheek and lip, robes tree and flower;
Where'er thy tiny globules press,
Each atom shines in loveliness.

Thou'rt beating in my brain and heart;
Oh, tell me whence and what thou art!
Vain questioning! e'en now, with speed
Thy ever-rolling waves recede.

And through my heart, subdued and slow,
The heavy feet of Sorrow go;
While brown Decay, with failing breath,
Leads in her pallid daughter, DEATH.

THE TIDE OF LIFE.

Oh, life! roll back thy sparkling wave!
Stranded, I tremble by the grave;
I stretch my freezing arms to plead;
Yet, still, thy mocking waves recede.

Oh, thou art pure and silver-white!
Art kindly, beautiful and bright!
Art healing as Bethsada's pool,
Art soft, and sweet, and dewy-cool!

An inlet from the flood divine;
And yet, ah, life! thou art not mine.
Adown my breast thy waters play,
And softly, slowly ebb away.

Slowly and softly — hush, my heart!
Let the last, loitering wave depart;
For, surely as its eddies go,
Another tide of life must flow.

Another tide; and, oh, how sweet!
Will rise, and lift thee from thy feet.
All silver-white, 'twill bear thee on,
And softly land thee at the THRONE.

THE LABORING MAN.

I like the honest laboring man!
    A soldier, brave and strong,
In the good war he leads the van —
    A worthy theme for song.

I like him, that he likes himself,
    And scorns to sink so low,
As to assoil his soul for pelf,
    Though pressed by want and woe.

I like him, that he wears no cloak
    To hide an inward ill;
But moves among all human folk,
    A human being still.

I like him for the love he bears
    His earnest, toiling wife —
A love, that lights her cloudiest cares,
    And glorifies her life.

I like him for the tender flower
  That blossoms on his cheek,
When he has used his willing power,
  To guard the small and weak.

Just such a man was he — my sire,
  With heart of giant bulk,
That would not leave the ship, though fire
  Had wrapped its sinking hulk.

Toiling, from morn till night, to send
  Grim poverty away;
An honest man — an ardent friend: —
  A Christian every day.

Twelve little spirits crowned his life:
  Beneath love's pleasant eyes,
Nine gird themselves for earthly strife,
  Three sought the peaceful skies.

Each birth brought added joy to him
  And added labor too; —
At every death his eyes grew dim,
  To find no more to do.

His wife — our mother — when he found
  Her weary, how he gave

His ready help, before a sound
    The little boon could crave.

Which of us can not say how much
    He loved us;—how his voice
Could soothe, and how his gentle touch
    Made the young heart rejoice?

In our young childhood's healthy bloom,
    Led by a wayward will,
We followed him from loom to loom,
    And wondered at his skill.

Pleased to receive his kind command—
    Of father patience full—
We learned, with slow, mistaking hand,
    To card the fleecy wool.

With gentle talk our thoughts he spun
    To threads, complete and strong;
And, by his careful skill begun,
    The web will wear us long.

One day (alas! that suns should glow,
    In spring o'er hill and vale,

And our life's autumn sunlight grow
　　So deadly cold and pale;)

He left his work — all slow and weak,
　　With frequent laboring sigh,
With drooping head and pallid cheek,
　　He sought our home to die.

With woe-worn hearts, a-near we came,
　　And circling, stood about,
To see love's mild and tender flame,
　　In death's dark wave go out.

Ah, me! the grave-king's icy breath
　　Had sudden deadly power.
Within the arctic land of death,
　　We planted life's fair flower.

And, as we turned away, we said,
　　With tears on heart and face,
Its holy perfume now was shed,
　　Within a kindlier place.

God bless the honest laboring man!
　　And sweeten all his toil!
Keep him from harboring selfish plan,
　　Or swelling wild turmoil.

And, when he gathers up his feet,
   And vails his blinding eyes,
Kind Father, give him labor sweet,
   In the seraphic skies.

DREAM-LAND.

Oh! home of the heart! if thy glad morning light
Can charm from my spirit the shadow of night,
Let me leave the dark world, e'er its cares shall o'erwhelm,
And linger awhile in thy song-haunted realm.

For the storm sweepeth by, and his wing is so dark,
I am weary of guiding my fragile life-bark;
Lo! worn out with toil, reason faints at the helm,
Let me linger awhile, in thy song-haunted realm.

Bright fancy, its monarch, shall guide me afar,
To the land where no storm-cloud my quiet can mar;
All day, from the cold world I'll linger apart,
In beautiful dream-land, the home of the heart.

My dull eye shall beam on the bluest of skies,
And the dew of sweet thought my worn spirit
    baptize;
And the sunlight of love, at my heart creeping in,
Shall chase far away the dark shadow of sin.

The gush of sweet music shall banish despair;
For the spirit of melody lingereth there;
And chastened and thrilled with her magic and
    might,
The heart of the dreamer grows wild with de-
    light.

Oh! visions of beauty! how sweetly ye rise,
In the bright land of dreams, to my wondering
    eyes!
And fairer than light are the scenes ye unfold,
As ye waft me along on your pinions of gold.

Oh! the care-laden world may be shrouded in
    night;
But dream-land is floating in music and light.
The dim eye gets brighter, the weak heart
    grows strong,
'Neath the sheen of its beauty, the chime of its
    song.

No music more soul-thrilling bliss can impart
Than the carol of fancy, that bird of the heart;
All graceful and pure, as a snowy-winged dove,
She soareth aloft in the sunlight of love.

DEW-DROPS OF KNOWLEDGE.

"Little flower, what dost thou,
With that coroneted brow,
Sitting, all the stilly eves,
Princess-like, 'mid courtier-leaves?"
  And the posie answered low;
  Or, at least, I fancied so;—
  "'T is my sole, sweet work to grow."

"Little birdie, stay and tell
Why, from out thy bosom's well,
Burst such rivulets of song;
Sure, such constant mirth is wrong!"
  "Nay!" said the melodious thing,
  As he flew on airy wing,
  "'T is a sacred joy to sing."

"Streamlet, in thy pathway pause;
Tell me all thy little laws.

Why do green leaves, at thy brink,
Scoop thy pearly wave to drink?"
   And the pretty streamlet laughed---
   "Hast thou, mortal, never quaffed
   Dewy love's delicious draught?"

Then I sat and mused awhile;
And I murmured with a smile,
"How the mind will strain to reach
Truths, that lowliest things can teach!
   Now, of verity, I know,
   While eternal suns shall glow,
   We shall sing, and love, and grow."

LIFE'S WARFARE.

It is a toilsome task to walk
    The straight and narrow way,
And tempters stand on every side,
    To lead the soul astray.

And oft, deceived by guileful words,
    The spirit will not heed
The warning voice, but walketh on,
    Where'er the tempters lead.

Pride thrills the foolish, wayward heart,
    With bitter, scornful tone,
Till love unfurls her snow-white wings,
    And leaves the soul alone.

Suspicion weaves her dark conceits,
    And cons them o'er and o'er,
Till heavenly faith, with golden robe,
    Walks with the soul no more.

Deceit, with hollow, harmful wiles,
    And heart of dark unrest,
Robs truth—bright seraph—of her home,
    Within the yeilding breast.

The fire that passion kindles there,
    Unsmothered by control,
Leaves purity no dwelling-place,
    Within the troubled soul.

And justice can not rule the heart
    Where jealousy hath sway;
And hatred, with her sneer and frown,
    Drives charity away.

Ah! the weak soul! it toileth on
    At warfare all the while;
On life's dark clouds it scarce can see
    The bow of promise smile.

Its firm resolves, its earnest hopes,
    Its yearnings after light,
Seem transient, as the idle words
    The winds do sing at night.

Still onward, onward to the grave,
    Its hurrying footsteps tend,

In mystery life's path begins;
    In mystery doth it end.

Yet not alone the soul doth go;
    Bright messengers of light,
Are walking with it day by day,
    To guide its steps aright.

And when the tempters have deceived,
    And led the soul astray,
Oh! tenderly they call it back,
    To walk the narrow way!

And, more than all, the Father's hand
    His erring child doth hold;
The loving Shepherd guardeth well
    The lambkin of the fold.

Then faint not, soul, that stumbleth on,
    A-weary and unblest;
A little while, thy Father's voice
    Shall summon thee to rest;

And then, within the pearly gates,
    Beside the tree of life,

How light a thing, amid thy bliss,
　Will seem thine earthly strife.

Joy to thee, then! a conqueror's crown
　Upon thy spirit-brow;—
What soul that dwelleth there, could be
　More sweetly blest than thou?

THE WIND.

The wind came over the hills one day,
    Singing a charming tune;
As light and low as the sleepy lay,
    Of a humming-bird in June.

I should not have heeded his idle song,
    But his breath was on my face,
And his arms around my neck were flung,
    In a fairy-like embrace.

Then, "Whither away, sweet wind?" said I;
    "And why is thy song so gay?
And why do thy waving pinions fly
    So busily all the day?"

"Like a child asleep," the zephyr said,
    "I have lain the whole long night,
With the moonbeams spread above my bed,
    For a covering, pure and white.

"But just as the sun from out of the sea
  Had lifted his princely head,
The morn, like a mother, lifted me
  From out of my snowy bed.

"Then, up, like a singing bird, I flew,
  O'er meadow and grassy hills;
I sprinkled the clover-heads with dew,
  Exhaled from a thousand rills.

"I gathered the lithe, gold, willow limbs,
  That hung so meekly down,
And drew them over the laughing streams
  In a beautiful, glossy crown.

"I swept the boughs of the beech aside,
  To look at the nestling birds;
The broken flower at the fountain's side,
  I cheered with my loving words.

"I fluttered around with the laughing hours,
  O'er forest and creeping vine;
I gleefully kissed the bending flowers,
  Till their lips were as red as wine.

"And thus I fly, o'er the rustling grass,
  And the wheat, on smiling farms,
Till the old nurse, Night, comes down at last,
  And cradles me in her arms."

Then, "Whither away?" said the wind to me,
  "And where hast thou been to-day?
And why is thy face so sad to see,
  When every thing else is gay?"

"Alas! sweet wind," I sighed to say,
  While the tears in my eyelids grew,
"I have not borne to a soul, to-day,
  A draught of the heart's cool dew.

"I have not searched for the broken flowers,
  That wither along my way;
Nor noted the flight of the priceless hours,
  Nor bent my knee to pray.

"But, oh! however my soul hath sinned,
  Thy lesson of love I'll keep;
Then, pass thou on, sweet, wandering wind,
  And leave me alone to weep."

PARTING.

Oh! sing to me some little song,
    Some tender and melodious air,
That through my brain shall glide along,
    And start low echoes there.
    Care, like Euroclydon,
Has chilled me through with driving sleet.
Oh! let thy voice, subdued and sweet,
Like summer-waves, on loitering feet,
Against my throbbing temples beat,
      Till all the pain is gone.

Forgetful of all dire mishap,
    Beneath the kindness of thy face,
I lay my head upon thy lap,
    And claim thy last embrace.
    While thou art o'er'me bowed,
I watch thy gentle loves arise,
And float and quiver in thine eyes,
Like the warm morning's shifting dyes,

When light first trembles in the skies,
    And smiles upon the cloud.

We part; and it may be for aye;
    None know the number of their years;
Ah! at that thought, thine eyes' soft day
    Is lost in twilight tears.
    Nay! be not grieving thus;
I did not mean for aye, sweet love,
Only as life's swift shuttles move,
Like silken threads apart we shove;
But, surely, He who leans above,
    Most kindly watches us.

And, when our parted lives are done,
    What heavenly rapture it will be
To know them woven into one
    By careful Deity.
    Call back thy vanished smile.
Let us, with sacred, reverent trust,
Sure that the ways of God are just,
And our bright love-links can not rust,
Be severed, darling, if we must;
    'Tis but a little while.

PARTING.

Then sing to me some gentle song,
   And round my neck thy white arms wind,
While tender thoughts — a holy throng —
   Float over thy pure mind,
   And flower within thine eyes,
As lilies in smooth waters grow;
And, lovingly entwined so,
It may be we shall feel the glow
Of angel loves, and sweetly know
   The strength of angel ties.

THE PRICE OF BLOOD.

That diamond-flashing scepter,
　　That regal robe of state,
Those halls of princely grandeur,
　　The dwellings of the great;

That crown, with jewels studded,
　　That shield of rare device;
Ah! who would wish to own them,
　　Who counts their fearful price?

Their price! within the nations,
　　Where thrones majestic stand,
The blood of murdered millions
　　Cries out from all the land.

And fearful wails at morning,
　　And prayers for death at night,

THE PRICE OF BLOOD.

Go up amid their scorning,
   Who reckon life so light.

Groans bitterly outbreaking,
   Woes that may not be told—
What are they to the rulers
   Who barter blood for gold?

The widow and the orphan
   May starve for lack of bread,
If but the lips of princes
   With daintiest food are fed.

Ho! ye of prophet vision,
   Who watch for coming things,
Is there no bolt of vengeance
   To strike these sordid kings?

See how their fierce oppression
   Is weighing down mankind!
See how the floods of anguish
   Roll o'er the human mind!

Is there no angel standing
   On the eternal shore,

Swearing, by earth and heaven,
That this shall be no more?

Ah! 'mid this tempest tumult,
My spirit, be thou calm!
There falls an answering whisper,
"Our God hath said, 'I AM.'"

THE WILLOW TREE.

The willow tree is a graceful thing;
Its boughs are light as a wild bird's wing.
Daintily, airily, to and fro,
Over the gliding waves they go,
Lowly laughing and whispering —
Oh! the willow tree is a graceful thing.

A fairy thing is the willow tree,
Tossing its slender arms in glee
Over the violets, white as snow,
Hiding their cheeks in the grasses low;
Swinging, waltzing, merry and free,
Oh! a fairy thing is the willow tree.

The willow tree is a thing of gloom —
Under it lies a darkened room;
And ever its boughs go to and fro,
Dropping tears on the mound below.
Room and mound are Beauty's tomb,
O! the willow tree is a thing of gloom.

The willow tree is a musical thing —
A harp with many a sweet-toned string;
And, while the breezes over it play,
This is its sweet, consoling lay:
"Thy dead in the courts of heaven sing."
Oh! the willow tree is a musical thing.

NATURE'S FEAST.

O'er all the smiling land,
    Sunlight is lying;
Sweetly, from strand to strand,
    Breezes are flying.

Down by the fettered feet
    Of the young grain,
Soundeth the music-beat
    Of the glad rain.

Over the meadows sweet,
    Streamlets are going;
Shining moons make the wheat
    Ripe for the mowing.

Earth is man's dwelling. Here
    By the feast spread,
Nature, God's almoner,
    Breaketh him bread.

Saying, "Come bond and free,
   Hungry and cold,
That which God giveth me
   I'll not withhold."

To her, from every place,
   Come great and small;
And she, with smiling face,
   Feedeth them all.

Let man reach forth and take
   That which she giveth;
It shall all labor make
   Sweet, while he liveth.

All the good laws of God
   Glad to obey,
Until heaven from the sod
   Calls him away.

OUR PLAYMATE'S GRAVE.

Beneath the cedar tree
   That swingeth to and fro
With every touch the wild winds give,
   As o'er the hills they go,

There lies an humble grave,
   Uncared for and alone;
No flowers are planted on the sod,
   And at the head no stone.

The hill on which it lies
   Slopes downward, steep and low,
And endeth in a tangled dell,
   Where sunshine can not go.

All day, a little sound,
   From out the vale beneath,
Comes stealing up the shadowy ground,
   To that abode of death.

A sound of moving trees,
  Of bubbling water-springs,
Comes, mingled with the hurried beat
  Of restless, quivering wings.

Long years ago, they laid
  Our playmate to his rest,
And planted there the cedar tree,
  That swingeth o'er his breast.

A wooden slab beneath,
  Unlettered, brown, and bare;
And for the rest the sunshine brings
  The sweet spring-beauties there.

And, if the rain-drop creep
  Into his curtained bed,
It matters not,— all things should weep,
  When such a boy is dead.

THE MUSIC OF THE SOUL.

There is a music, soft and low,
    That dwelleth in the soul,
And ever there in secresy,
    Its untaught numbers roll.

It hath no words; but, oh, it bears
    The raptured soul along,
As though the atmosphere around
    Were tremulous with song.

It hath a wilder, sweeter sound,
    Than all earth's melodies,
As it were wafted to the heart,
    Adown the solemn skies.

And, like a far off anthem swell,
    It chimeth ever there;
And on its unseen wing it bears
    The burden of a prayer.

All through the long and weary day
  Its dreamy murmurs flow,
Chanting afar, within the soul,
  A requiem sad and low.

The eye may flash with angry light;
  The lip wear falsehood's smile;
Yet the sad music of the soul
  Swells softly all the while.

Forever sweeping through the breast
  These holy breathings are,
Like the low surging melodies
  That roll from star to star.

When night, devout and dewy eyed,
  Calls the lone soul to prayer,
All earthly numbers melt away,
  Like discord on the air.

And in its dim cathedral sits
  The dark and troubled soul,
And wondering, hears through nave and aisle,
  Its own wild music roll.

Oh! very dear, to earth-worn hearts,
 Are these sweet, heaven-born lays!
They quicken every wearied pulse,
 And rouse to love and praise.

THE CHRISTENING.

The moonlight trembled in the silvery air;
The wind sang in the woodbine by the door;
And the young mother, swaying in her chair,
Her tender lullaby crooned o'er and o'er.

"Sleep, my beautiful, sleep!
Evening shadows are deep.
Close in my arms I fold you,
Softly praying, with tears,
That the Father of all may hold you;—
Through all life's shadowy years,
Lovingly fold and keep,
Sleep, my beautiful, sleep!

"Sleep, my beautiful, sleep!
None but a mother would weep
O'er a babe as yet unchristened;—
O'er a bud as yet unblown;

Ere baptism-rains have glistened,
   In pearl-showers over it thrown;
   For the worm in the heart I weep:—
Sleep, my beautiful, sleep!"

The moonlight darkened in the draperied night,
The wind sobbed through the woodbine with a sigh,
And by a marble face, all still and white,
The mother wailed her tremulous lullaby.

   "Sleep, my beautiful, sleep!
   The shadows of death are deep.
Out of my arms they take you,
   Gird you in linens clean,
And never disturb or awake you.
   What can this slumber mean?
   Terrors over me creep,
   Sleep, my beautiful, sleep!

   "Sleep, my beautiful, sleep!
   Angels your christening keep;
And the worm can never harm you,
   That lies in the budding heart.

But what to my arms can charm you,
 When death has drawn us apart?
 They have opened the grave so steep;
 Sleep, my beautiful, sleep!"

OH! WOULD I WERE ALONE.

Oh! would I were alone!
For a dancing wind hath blown,
Throughout the shadowy forest of my soul;
And all its dreams, like trees,
Awake to melodies,
That lightly, lightly roll.
Oh! would we were alone!
I, and my happy soul.

Soft summer light hath shone,
Like a sweet benison,
Where chilling, wintry shadows long have lain;
I weary of the sound
Of the gossiping around;
The laughter quick and vain.
Oh! would we were alone—
I, and my luminous brain!

A new delight hath grown,
Like a white flower blown,

When the lessening snow-hills shrink apart,
　Within the sacred clime,
　Where I keep tryst with Time,
　　Yet mock his feeble art.
　Oh! would we were alone—
　I, and my charmed heart!

　Oh! the dancing wind hath blown,
　　And summer light hath shone,
Through my soul's forest, shadowy and deep,
　　And such a fairy throng
　　Awaits me, that I long
　　　My sacred tryst to keep.
　　Oh! would I were alone—
　　To muse and smile and weep.

PRAYER AND PRAISE.

When, in the heart, the tide of woe
  Is swelling every hour;
When heavy eye and pallid brow
  Reveal its fearful power;

When lips are mute, because the brain
  Can frame, of speech, no form;
When outward calmness only shows
  How wild the inward storm;

Then, even as the tortured wave
  Wails forth its deep despair,
So the wrung heart sends up the voice
  Of earnest, pleading prayer.

When peace within the happy breast
  Doth like a river flow,
And gladly, through the heart and vein,
  Health's gentle currents go;

When dreams, like birds, float lightly through
   The brain, on golden wing,
And tarry just enough to breathe
   The strange, sweet songs they sing.

Then, even as the gushing stream
   Doth chant its joyous lays,
So swells from out the raptured heart,
   Its glad, spontaneous praise.

Sweet prayer! the child of faith and love,
   Whose holy accents rise,
In lowest music tones, yet find
   Their echo in the skies;

And praise — outgushing of a heart,
   That God hath greatly blessed,
The pean of delight that swells,
   In triumph from the breast;

Ye both, with holy influences,
   Gird the repentant soul,
That it may run the heavenward race,
   And reach the sun-crowned goal.

THE DYING TEACHER.*

    Smitten, with sore disease,
He lies — a student, who has climbed so high
Earth's stony "hill of science" that his eye
    No higher station sees;

    But peers into the night
That girds the mountain on the skyward side,
Expecting, when its raven clouds divide,
    To view some fairer hight.

    Life, like a book well worn,
And diligently conned in youth and age;
Death, the stern master, opens at a page,
    The last, defaced and torn.

---

* The last words of an aged schoolmaster were, "It is growing dark; school may be dismissed."

THE DYING TEACHER.

Slowly the pale lips stir,
(Once crimson altars where thought-offerings
burned,)
As if the lessons were but slightly learned,
And so forgotten were.

His words are strange and few;
Yet even in this hour of mortal pain,
Memory, the slumberer, wakes, and turns again
The pages, for review.

Ah! first the pictured book,
Did his sweet mother open to his sight;
And, at his eager boyhood's rapt delight,
Smiling, she bade him look.

Gently, as unfledged dove,
He nestled in her arms, the while she read;
With weak, uncertain lips his lesson said,
His mother-lore of love.

The winged years went and came
All radiantly. He hardly felt their flight,
For that dear smile, which made, with rainbow
light,
Life's bubbles all aflame.

THE DYING TEACHER.

Till, in youth's sunny prime,
Another hand turned o'er the glowing leaves,
And taught his soul the tales that fancy weaves,
In music-gliding rhyme.

As silvery-vested dawn
Lightly precedes the vital, vigorous day,
When fancy's gilded shallop cut the way,
Love in its wake was drawn.

'Twas but the common lot;
He loved, and suffered; so he learned that life
Is like a book with mournful chapters rife,
And soiled with many a blot.

And thus, impatient grown
To master all life's mysteries at a bound,
With passionate hand he swept the leaves, and
found
Dread language, and unknown.

Ah! sadly then he learned
That time unravels but the present page,
And toil must every mystic line engage,
Or ere a leaf be turned.

And, finding grief in store,
And bitter truths with sad precision taught,
Forsook wild dreams; and, on the waves of
    thought,
    His sinking soul upbore.

    Where mystery's ocean sweeps,
He sought creation's rare and hidden things;
Soul-gems that make men wealthier than kings,
    He gathered from her deeps.

    And, then, with kingly grace,
(For most a king is honored if he stoop,)
He took the golden chain of knowledge up,
    And bound him to his race.

    A teacher—scorning not
Along with little souls to tread once more
The simple, tiresome paths of infant lore,
    Nor murmured at his lot.

    Oh, meek, unselfish heart!
To see fame's regal mountain towers alight,
With pathway thitherward all smooth and
    bright,
    And act such humble part.

THE DYING TEACHER

Prone on his couch he lies,
Life's twilight shadows gather o'er his brow,
And the warm, loving light is fading now,
From out his half-closed eyes.

The night is chill and whist—
The long, drear night that reigns among the dead.
"'T is growing dark," the gentle spirit said,
"And school may be dismissed."

We can not see the book
Whose golden letters satisfy the soul;
But we, when earth is shriveled like a scroll,
Shall on its pages look;

And there all wisdom learn,
All love, all beauty, all divinity.
Oh, happy teacher! to be taught like thee,
What spirit would not yearn!

SONG.

I love every thing beautiful,
    Every thing pure and true;
The wild flower's purple corolla,
    Vailed with a 'broidering dew.

The gleam of a curling wavelet,
    The shape of a curious leaf,
That broadens out of its petiole,
    Charmeth away my grief.

I love every thing musical—
    Murmur of zephyr and wave,
Voices of nature solemn
    As dirges over a grave.

The sweep of a forest pinion,
    The rustle of woodland limb,
Steal over the troubled spirit,
    Like the gush of a prayerful hymn.

But, oh! the fullness of beauty
  Lies couched in a soullit eye,
When I see, 'neath the lifted lashes,
  A love that can not die.

And of all things full of music,
  Nought maketh my heart rejoice,
Or waketh an answering echo,
  Like the sound of a loving voice.

THE FLOWER LANGUAGE OF THE HEART.

With my hands endowed with pansies,
   Plucked in dreamy, pleasant mood,
Blossoming into flowery fancies,
   Near the garden bower I stood.

Then I heard a little singing,
   From within, arise and fly,
Through the leaves its slow way winging,
   Half a song, and half a sigh.

" Through my heart's lone garden stealing,
   Filled with memories of the past,
Mourned I for the flowers of feeling,
   Withered at life's wintry blast.

"Once, the sweet wild roses bowered,
   This fair dwelling of my heart;
And the lowly violet flowered,
   Guiltless of deceiving art.

"And the rosy almond-blossoms,
  With a smile of hope for me,
Hung with warm and throbbing bosoms,
  O'er the rapt anemone.

"Long ago they grew and withered,
  And my eyes are full of tears,
As if grief her dews had gathered
  Out of all those pleasant years.

"Bars of light the green leaves silvered,
  Glorying all my fairy bowers;
But the days, deceitful, pilfered,
  One by one, my precious flowers.

"Wandering up in careless vagrance,
  To my gleeful childhood's close;
Then my soul was filled with fragrance,
  By the beautiful white rose.

"Soon it faded; brown and dusky
  Fell its shriveled leaves apart;
And the tempest voice was husky
  O'er this garden of my heart.

"Crimson rosebuds, just out-starting,
    To an ashen pallor grew;
And Adonis' blooms were parting,
    Near the sad disdainful rue.

"Crowned with mocking thistle-flowers,
    Underneath the Judas tree,
Sighing for the summer bowers,
    That would bloom no more for me.

"Thus, through my heart's garden stealing,
    Filled with memories of the past,
Grieved I for the flowers of feeling,
    Withered at life's wintry blast.

"But there rose a blossom starry,
    And its mystic language said,
'Wherefore by the snowdrift tarry?
    Rise! to Bethlehem be led.'

"From my blissful Eden driven,
    Praying for a swift release,
Came a snowy dove from heaven,
    With the olive branch of peace.

"Round my forehead angel fingers
  Bound the wreath with nimble art,
And a holy presence lingers
  Evermore within my heart."

With my hands endowed with pansies,
  Down the garden path I walked,
Blossoming into flowery fancies,
  Thus unto my soul I talked:

"When a little bud is blowing,
  All too early in the spring,
Wild winds hinder it from growing,
  Chilling mists around it cling.

"And the plant that feels the rigor
  Of the spring-time frost and gloom,
Is not warmed with half the vigor
  Of the crimson summer bloom.

"Now I think this human flower
  Was but chilled a little while;
That in August sun and shower
  It might all the brighter smile.

"So, if in the soul a sadness
   Seems to chill the springs of life,
Let us wait with patient gladness,
   Bliss is heralded by strife."

THE BIRD AND THE HEART.

    Fly, fly,
Beautiful bird into the sky!
  While your carols, like jewels fine,
  Drop and dissolve in the air's pure wine,
  That sparkles and swims in the light divine,
Of the sun-god's beatific eye,
    Fly, fly!
Mate with the clouds that are hurrying by.

    Lave, lave
Your azure wings in its slow, warm wave!
  And fill your trachea, gleeful one,
  Till the delicate pipe shall overrun,
  And you end the song your flight begun,
With a higher, clearer, merrier stave,
    Lave, lave,
In the blissful flow of the ambient wave.

    Sink, sink!
The rubric light has paled to pink,

And amber and lavender, white and gold,
Bewilder the sea, and trouble the mold;
For the garlanded day is growing old,
And totters along to the sunset brink.
    Sink, sink!
Till the shade of the cold, still night shall shrink.

    Heart, heart,
Up to the higher glories dart!
    Heaven's most holy beams are thine;—
    Burst into song in the light divine;—
    Drink deep draughts of the soul's rare wine,
Then sink till death's terrorful night, shall depart.
    Heart, heart!
Trustfully sleep till the night shall depart.

AN INVALID'S DREAM.

Tears from kind eyes over me falling,
  Tender arms enclosing me round;
And a troubled voice, in words appalling,
  Smiting my ear with swords of sound:—
    "Never, never to be well!"
    Never more to feel the swell,
    Of healthy girlhood's bounding wave,
    All my sentient being lave,
    Till I drop into my grave.

"Alas! for the beautiful things denied me!
  Joy in the light, and rest in the shade,
Love to linger entranced beside me;
  Weakness, to cling to my arm for aid."
    Thus I cried within my soul;
    Then, I felt above me roll
    Clouds of rest; and, for a term,
    Slumbers shrouding folds were firm,
    As the cocoon round the worm.

AN INVALID'S DREAM.

Was it a dream? or was I but daunted,
   With semblance of what was bitterly true?
In the swift seas my feet were planted,
   And the wild waters around me grew.
     Puny sport of wind and sea,
     Did I seem that hour to be;—
     Of the rolling surge afraid,
     Lifted I my voice, and prayed,
     With a sob, for instant aid.

Then, a black storm-cloud over me parted,
   To roll in a whitening scroll afar;
And a voice, all melody, cried, "Faint-hearted;
   See where the steadfast islands are!"
     Much I wondered, and behold!
     In a flood of shimmering gold,
     Lay a bright land near to me,
     Crowned with all things fair to see,
     Girt with shining marquetry.

Down, amid bursting light was tendered,
   A hand, milk-white, and slender and fair;
Then was my languishing spirit rendered
   Strong to resist, and brave to dare.
     Joyously the tide I pressed,

Eager for the promised rest,
Guided by the loving hand,
Till a-near the blissful strand,
Back withheld by strange command.

"Wait! little child! and ponder a season!
　Lovely as this fair land may be,
Is there not yet some secret reason,
　Why you should buffet the angry sea?"
　　All the green and cumbrous trees,
　　Stood, like palaces of ease;
　　And the long vines o'er them wound,
　　Reeling to the fruitful ground,
　　With a pleasant, summery sound.

All the bright valleys were overladen,
　And shining with flowers, rose-tinted and
　　　rare;
And many a blooming youth and maiden
　Wandered together, with laughter, there.
　　Full of earnest, doubtful thought,
　　With an eye, by suffering taught,
　　Questioned I their ways to see,
　　If untangled, smooth and free,
　　Every blooming course might be.
9

Then I shook like a smitten reed to view it,
  With exquisite wonder and exquisite fear;
Deadly serpents were winding through it;
  O'er scarlet blossoms I saw them veer.
    Where the heedless legion stepped,
    Many a filthy quagmire slept;
    Clouds that seemed but "as a hand,"
    Gathering wrathfully and grand,
    Smote to death the smiling land.

Poison, in every good was lurking;
  Thorns were hidden on every spray;
And the ghostly phantoms of night were working
  Up through the long bright halls of day.
    Then I wept awhile, and said,
    "Little have I merited,
    Lord, thy sweet, protecting care;
    Once again the seas I dare,
    Only love and keep me there.

"Little of faith! the gathering billow,
  No more thy purified soul can chafe;
I lead thee under the drooping willow,
  Grateful the shade, and cool and safe!"

Then the fair hand went away;
And beneath the tree I lay,
Tearful, pallid, but no more,
Frighted at the hungry roar
Of the sea beyond the shore.

Then, in my soul, there grew a wonder;
  For the sweet land that cherished me,
From the broad aisle was rent asunder,
  And drifted away across the sea.
    All the wave hills grew with speed,
    Level as a summer mead;
    And the swinging branches flew,
    With articulation new,
    Saying, "Heaven is just in view."

Faces unearthly over me gleaming;—
  Harpings, most heavenly charming my ear;
Panting and blissful I woke from dreaming,
  Just as the symphonies clustered near.
    "Never—never to be well!"
    Where the wild seas beat and swell,
    Swayed about, yet now I see,
    To the singing willow tree,
    My Physician leadeth me.

THE THREE BIRDLINGS.*

A STORY FOR LITTLE ONES.

Come Nellie, and Mina, and Mary,
   Sweet sisters of mine, come near;
For I have a beautiful story
   To tell, as you ever did hear.

A story of three little birdlings,
   All born in the beauteous May;
So what will you give me, my darlings,
   To sing you my story to-day?

"A hundred and fifty sweet kisses?"
   That can not be worth your while,

---

*I have, in this article, been guilty of misrepresenting the habits of some of the feathered tribes, inasmuch as the brown thrush builds his nest on the ground, and the chick-a-dee, and blue-bird, have a most unpoetical attachment to stumps and "stubs;" but I think, for the purposes of versification, the liberty may be excused.

For I shall be paid for my trouble,
  If you give me but one sweet smile.

But stand at my side while I draw you
  A bucket up, out of my well;
The well of my love for you, sisters,
  Much deeper than story can tell.

There were three little nests in the woodland,
  Built carefully up out of reach;
One swung in a small witchhazel,
  And two in a lofty beech.

If you had climbed to them in April,
  In each of them, you might have seen
Little eggs, either prettily spotted,
  Or tinted with delicate green.

Well, when the bright May was a-laughing,
  And shaking her curls in the sun;
Of featherless, tiniest birdlings,
  In each of the nests, there was one;

For whether the rain had rained on them,
  Or some wicked boy had been there,

Or whether some owlet had killed them,
   I can not this moment declare;

But, certain it is, there was only
   A bird, at the last, in each nest,
That stretched up its neck for the feeding,
   And slept 'neath the motherly breast.

Now, when the June came, with a mantle
   Of gold, all embroidered with green,
The birdlings, grown feathered and larger,
   Began to look out on the scene.

And waving their light, downy pinions,
   And hopping from this bough to that,
They happened to meet altogether,
   And stopped for a neighborly chat.

Says one, "I make bold to acquaint you,
   'T is little Miss Blue-bird you see."
Says another, "Your servant, Miss Blue-bird,
   And I am Miss Chick-a-dee-dee.

"But step just a little one side, dear,
   The better our voices to hush;—

I am told that this brownie, beside us,
  Is nobody — only Miss Thrush.

"Now, if this should be true, dear Miss Blue-
    bird,
  'Tis best we should 'cut' her you know;
For 'they say' that the 'family-tree,' love,
  Is very decidedly 'low;'

And besides, without any more bother,
  Her 'quality,' truly to guess —
She is certainly lacking in style, love —
  Just look at the cut of her dress!"

"Indeed!" said the dainty Miss Blue-bird,
  As her delicate wings she unfurled,
"Let us hurry away, for I wouldn't
  Be seen by her side, for the world.

"For, when I 'come out,' I shall glisten
  In colors so pretty and rich,
That I'm certain to capture the red-breast,
  Or blue-jay, I can not tell which.

"And, if I should own her acquaintance,
  That scornful Miss Black-bird would fly,

And sound it all over creation,
   To every bird in the sky."

Now, little Miss Thrush, the poor "brownie,"
   Had heard every word that they said;
While the thought of her lowly condition
   Crept into her wondering head.

And the dress that she wore looked so shabby,
   (Though 't was really tidy and plain,
Just such a dark tint as a lady
   Would choose to wear out in the rain,)

That while, to their nests in the beech tree,
   She saw the pert misses depart,
Away, to her humble witch-hazel,
   She went with a sorrowful heart.

Saying, "Now, I will stay here forever,
   Out of sight of the chick-a-dee-dee;
And never a red-breast, or blue-jay,
   Shall perch in my family-tree."

Now gone was the sweet lady-summer;
   And gone was the winter so wild;

And April came back to the woodland,
　As bright as a beautiful child.

And shining in delicate azure,
　Miss Blue-bird "came out" as she said,
And Miss Chick-a-dee-dee looked about her,
　And thought it was high time to wed.

So she sang out, "My charming Miss Blue-bird,
　Since you are so bright and so gay,
And withal, so 'accomplished' and stylish,
　You're certain to capture the jay.

"But, I hear that the red-breast is partial
　To something less gaudy and smart;
So I've put on my quakerish mantle,
　And mean he shall sue for my heart."

Now, the thrush in her lowly witchhazel,
　(Grown older and wiser, you see,)
When she heard this absurd calculation,
　Could not forbear laughing with glee.

Her laughing gushed out in such music,
　That all the bright birds in a throng,

Hurried into the echoing woodland,
  To list to the wonderful song.

For never in concert or solo
  Was any thing heard so complete,
So gleeful, so richly delicious,
  So mellow, so tenderly sweet.

"Oh! who can it be?" cried the black-bird;
  And "who can it be?" squalled the jay;
Said the red-breast, "Be still with your screech-
     ing!
  You'll frighten the lady away."

Each crying aloud in his wonder,
  And telling the others to hush.
Lo! out of the humble witchhazel
  Came down the brown wings of the thrush.

"Oh! sweet, I'm delighted to see you!"
  Sang out the glib chick-a-dee-dee;
"My charming Miss Thrush," said the blue-bird,
  "Come stay with us, up in our tree."

"Our set are all dying to know you,
  Where have you been hidden away?

My neighbor, Miss Thrush, Mr. Red-breast,
   A friend of mine, good Mr. Jay."

But gaily she laughed, as she answered,
   "My pretty young belles, do you know
That my 'family-tree,' the witchhazel,
   'Is very decidedly low?'

"So I dare not fly up to your beech-tree,
   Though obliged to you, nevertheless,
Do n't you see that I 'm 'lacking in style,' dears!
   Just look at the cut of my dress!"

Then back to her lowly witchhaze
   She flew, with a carol of glee,
Singing, "No, I will never forsake you —
   My cherishing 'family-tree.'"

Now, Nellie, and Mina, and Mary,
   If any one seem to look down
With sneers, on your name and your station,
   Or scoffs at the cut of your gown,

Never mind it, my sweet little sisters,
   Or rail at the world for its pride;

They have but their beauty, or riches,
   And you may have something beside:

A voice that is gushing with music,
   A heart that is brimming with glee,
A mind full of wisdom, are better
   Than any tall "family-tree."

And if the bright world shall be startled,
   Some day, by the power of your song,
And feed you with honey-regard, dears,
   Let flattery do you no wrong.

But lift up your light, little pinions,
   And away to the olden delight;
For the loves that are made by the fashion,
   Are the loves that are surest in flight.

HAPPY DAYS.

When we have been in with the roses,
   And pressed their cool faces to ours,
Long after, around us will linger
   The subtle, faint odor of flowers.

Even so, when life leadeth us onward,
   O'er dreary and desert-like ways,
Kind memory, like a sweet perfume,
   Recalleth our flower-like days.

When we have been out in the sunshine,
   And dwelt in the glow of its light,
The warmth of its presence surrounds us,
   Beneath the cold wings of the night.

Glad days are like sunbeams that cheer us;
   Like sunbeams they also depart;
Yet, passing, they kindly bequeath us
   The warmth of their light in the heart.

The way of the world may be stony,
  (Alas, who has found it not so!)
Yet, now and then, Time, leaning o'er us,
  Drops pearls in our path, as we go.

Then let us thank God, as we travel,
  Heart-wearily, on to our rest,
For the sunshine, the pearls, and the roses
  That make our dark pilgrimage blest.

LIGHT.

The meek morning twilight, so paley of hue,
   Whose face was so pearl-white, whose brow was so grand,
Sweeping by with strong influence, after her drew
   The glad waves of sunshine all over the land.

Like a sea-surge, yet silent withal, o'er the pines
   And the mountains they rolled; the green vallies ran o'er;
And the edges of all things wore dainty white lines,
   As the light billows foamed on each glorified shore.

There came such a murmur from hollow and dell,
   A sound with all silences so blended in,
So slumberous-quiet, you scarcely could tell,
   Were it sunshine or breeze that was making the din.

The soft air swam backward and forward to see
  Who had lain such a sweet weight of sound
    on her breast;
Yet went she all softly, lest rosebush and tree,
  At the noise of her swimming, should wake
    from their rest.

The tremulous eddy encircled the glade,
  And touched the pale lips of the flowers in
    the wood;
Yet moved not the line of the quaintly-marked
    shade,
  And stirred not the slenderest stem as they
    stood.

There was something a-move, all along the
    hushed world;
  It rocked the low grasses, it girdled the
    boughs;
It breathed, and the folded young leaflets un-
    curled,
  While the trees, like robed bishops, were
    paying their vows.

It breathed—I know not if it uttered a word;
  (It must be, the leaf-buds have daintier ears,)

But all living things with the presence were
    stirred,
  As if they had heard some sweet voice of the
    spheres.

They answered, but softly ; I heard the reply,
  "Oh, spirit of blessedness! circling us so,
With the warmth of thine heart and the glow
    of thine eye,
  In the joy of thy presence, we grow—and
    WE GROW!

And the sound of their growing, albeit as faint
  As the star-hymns that down through the
    distances fall,
On my heart, that had long been so full of
    complaint,
  Lay in music power — hushing its murmur-
    ings all.

And such a sweet calm came upon me that hour;
  So stilly the passion-tide sank to its ebb,
Bliss-trembling, I felt with the leaf-bud and
    flower,
  The PRESENCE encircle my soul like a web.

And such a perception — a musical sense —
  That seemed of the Infinite surely a part,
Came to me, that softly, I can not say whence,
  The voice of the PRESENCE crept into my heart.

It spoke of the wonder, the grandeur of LAW;
  It talked of the love that constrains to obey;
It said, while I kneeled, over-burdened with awe,
  "The coming of love is the dawning of day."

Wide open the doors of my spirit I threw,
  And let the glad waves of the sunshine inroll;
In the joy of their surging, I grew — and I grew —
  For love was the light that had dawned on my soul.

THE MESSENGER.

A sorrow stole o'er me —
　All swiftly it stole,
And darkly it shadowed
　My brow and my soul.

My heart's happy summer
　Went by with its mirth;
Its rose-blooms of pleasure
　Were crushed to the earth.

Alone, in the winter,
　Dismayed and forlorn,
I looked for no gladness;
　I hoped for no morn.

Where lo! through the darkness,
　Stole glimpses of day;
And the wing of an angel
　Flashed over my way

Oh! never heard mortal
  Such music before :
"The Father hath sent me;
  Thy trial is o'er."

How passed the lone winter,
  So darksome and wild!
The beautiful summer—
  How sweetly it smiled!

Like a terrible vision,
  The shadow went by,
'Neath the smile of the Father—
  OUR Father on high.

WHO KNOWETH THE HEART!

Oh! oft are we told of warriors bold
   Who led, with a look, the yielding throng;
And the mournful fate of the good and great
   Is chanted in many a funeral song.

And oft do we read of their terrible need,
   Who writhe under poverty's keenest smart,
And the rich grew pale at the sorrowful tale;
   But who hath written the life of the heart?

Oh! who can tell if the heart's dark cell
   Is thrilling with pleasure or throbbing with pain!
For the glance will be gay, when its hopes steal away,
   All silent and sad like a funeral train.

Who knoweth the theme of the heart's fond dream,
   In the lingering twilight, holy and still!

Who counteth its tears and telleth its fears,
   When sorrow broods o'er it heavy and chill!

Oh, the world hath no part in the life of the heart!
   Unmarked are its conflicts, unheeded its woes;
It dwelleth alone, its conquests unknown,
   And its deep wells of feeling, ah! who shall disclose!

Though the cloud of dismay hath rolled over its way,
   In its pride and its anguish it throbeth apart;
The glance may be bright when it dwelleth in night,
   And God, alone, knoweth the life of the heart.

THE DEATH OF THE OLD YEAR.

The old, white-headed year
  Went murmuring to his rest,
And many a frozen tear
  Fell on his snowy vest.

He shook his palsied head
  With a glance that chilled my heart,
And he pointed to the dead
  That were of his spoils a part.

And, as the cold wind played
  With the locks on his pallid brow,
" My life is o'er," he said ;
  " The sepulchre waits me now."

His voice, like the night-wind shrill,
  Rang wofully on mine ear ;
And I paused, while, murmuring still,
  He crept to his frozen bier.

"And dost thou weep for me?"
 'T was thus I heard him say;
"I shed no tears for thee,
 When I stole thy gems away.

"I have plucked thy fairest flowers,
 And hid them from thy sight;
And o'er thy gayest hours
 Have thrown a withering blight.

"I found thee, wild with glee,
 I leave thee, deathly sad;
I have not spared to thee
 One joy to make thee glad.

"My hand, amid thy cups,
 Has turned their wine to gall;
And from thy heart thy hopes,
 Like rose corollas, fall.

"Then wherefore weep for me?"
 The old year moaning said;
"The new year comes with glee;
 Rejoice when I am dead."

THE DEATH OF THE OLD YEAR.

With downcast, aching eyes,
   Beside his frozen bier,
Beneath the midnight skies,
   I watched the dying year.

The chill night-wind arose,
   And o'er the deep skies stole,
Wafting a cloud of woes,
   As dark as my own soul.

Down from the sable spheres,
   With wild, funereal cries,
Came a long train of years,
   And closed the rayless eyes.

And, with a heart like lead,
   I whispered, o'er the bier,
"Would that I, too, were dead
   And cold, like this dead year."

HEAVEN.

Land of the holy, sweet country of rest!
   Oh, tell me how far may thy boundaries be!
   Is there no bower in thy borders for me?
Have I not also some part with thy blest,
Land of the beautiful, country of rest?

I have been told of thy wonderful light,
   Glowing and flowing down from the Supreme;
   I have been told of thy life-giving stream,
Bordered so sweetly with flowers of white;
Kingdom of loveliness, home of delight.

Well do I know that the summers I love
   Dwell there forever, unshadowed by gloom;
   Royal their presence, unfading their bloom:
Fain would my spirit thy loveliness prove,
Fountain of happiness, dwelling of love.

Yet, were thy beauty but tinsel and glare;
   Yet, were thy summers unwelcome and cold,

Did I not know that thy sunshine of gold
Smiles o'er the loved ones who wait for me
    there,
Clad in the garments the cherubim wear.

Oh! let thick darkness rest over my head;
    Let dull-visaged care bear contentment away;
    Across my sad soul flies thy vision of day;
And faith to my heart's secret altar is led,
With peace, sweet consoler, eternally wed.

Sweet heaven! the thought of thy blessedness
    falls
    Upon me, like rain from the river of Life;
    And out of time's bitterness, out of its strife,
My soul, like a bird, in the fierce tempest calls
For rest by the side of thy sheltering walls.

THE LESSON.

Don't be frightened, little bird!
But your chirping voice I heard
Underneath the apple tree;
And I said, "I'll go and see;"
Thinking I perhaps might find
Some new lesson for the mind.

I'll be careful! ah! indeed,
Here's a family to feed,
And who does it? surely you
Must have something else to do.
Songs to sing, and sights to see —
What a burden they must be!

"Only four of them?" I know;
But the four must live and grow;
And your little wings must ply
To and fro, throughout the sky.

Don't you often think, my dear,
You have one too many here?

"Slander you?" You're very pert!
Surely, friend, I meant no hurt;
But it's very plain to see
You're as poor as bird can be
Every thing you seem to lack,
Save the little on your back.

Now, how can you sit and sing?
Really, such a fluttering
Makes me nervous. What a crowd!
How the piping, shrill and loud,
Must annoy you! yet, you seem
Cool and tranquil while they scream.

"Like to hear it?" Well, that's droll!
One who claims to have a soul
Said, but yesterday, to me,
"Never raise a family!"
But the matter let us hush —
'T was a woman — don't you blush?

Does it never, never prove
Wearisome, this mother-love?
When the golden days invite
To a higher, longer flight,
Does the heart forget its mirth—
Drooping, like the wing, to earth?

Ah! I hear your glad reply—
Hear it in your happy cry,
While I softly go away,
"Even for a single day,
Burden such as this to bear,
Is a bliss beyond compare."

Well, good by! when next you see
Some young lady, just like me —
Tell her over, word for word,
The sweet story I have heard,
Possibly, she *dare* not be
Burdened with a family.

Tell her how you gladly soar
After treasures for the four;
Tell her how you softly fling
Over them your guardian wing,
And like me, she 'll soon depart,
With a lesson for the heart.

VISIONS.

When silent-footed evening draws,
   With fingers cold and damp,
A curtain round the bustling earth,
   And lights her silver lamp,

Then, clustering round the weary heart,
   Come visions strange and fair;
And till the twilight hour is passed,
   They lightly linger there.

And, softly calling up again
   The forms of faded years,
Until the lip is pale, and eyes
   Are dim with gathering tears,

Among the chambers of the soul,
   Their gentle footsteps fall;
And holy hopes and high resolves
   Come thronging at their call.

They sing of love, and gentler grows
   The heart beneath their spell,
Till music gushes, soft and sweet,
   From chords they touch so well.

And ever after lurks a chime
   Amid its many cells,
Like the low winds imprisoned close
   Within the ocean shells.

They sing of death — the spirit thrills
   In sudden, deadly fear;
As thoughts of the long shroud arise,
   The coffin and the bier.

And silent tears fall down the breast;
   We feel a nameless dread,
As memory, pointing to the past,
   Calls up to us the dead.

Then come the friends we buried once,
   With earnest voices calling,
While the dark vail that hid them long
   From our rapt sight is falling.

And earth looks very cold and dark—
  And heaven looks bright and fair;
And the half-broken, restless heart
  Is longing to be there.

'Tis thus that twilight visions come,
  Laden with hope and light;
And sing the gladdened soul asleep,
  Beneath the brow of night.

THE FUTURE.

I stand on a barren shore,
   With the present at my side;
But, dreaming, I see, o'er the waves before,
   The years of the future glide.

I watch with eager eyes
   Those mystical years to be;
While the sweeping life-tide bears them on,
   As the ships are borne at sea.

The life-tide brings them on,
   Unharmed by breaker or blast;
But around me lie on my spirit-strand
   The wrecks of the desolate past.

The sad waves at my feet
   Break into a grievous moan;
But, afar, the songs of billows swell
   To a grand, triumphal tone.

THE FUTURE.

I will not heed the words,
    That the lone waves tell to me:
But my heart shall beat to the martial tune
    That surges across the sea.

I will not mourn the past—
    The present will soon depart;
Life's storms may wreck the passing years;
    But they shall not wreck my heart.

Perchance, some golden year,
    Like a ship, wide-winged and free
Will yet, all laden with blissful days,
    Float over the smiling sea.

And the grand, triumphal song
    That the far-off billows sing,
May be but a presage, glad and sweet,
    Of the joy those days shall bring.

So, thus, on the shore I'll stand,
    By the side of the swelling sea;
And, dreaming, wait till the tide shall bring,
    The mystical years to be.

TO A LITTLE POETESS.

Sing away, sweet Lottie, sing away!
   In this bustling kingdom of the world,
Many a voice is hushed that should be gay;
   Many a wing that ought to soar is furled.

Sing away, and be the robin's song
   Thine — outgushing from a happy heart,
Innocent of vanity and wrong —
   Learn of love and light thy music-art.

Never wish to be the nightingale;
   For the owl, (speak low, the critic, dear,)
Wakening at her voice in starlight pale,
   Hoots, "reviews" into her shrinking ear.

In the night of sorrow's bitterness,
   Richest, rarest poet strains are sent
From the secret spirit's dim recess,
   On the wailing wind of discontent.

TO A LITTLE POETESS.

Never wish to be the nightingale!
  Sing away, sweet Lottie, in the sun!
If thy crimson summer day should fail,
  Cease thy tune; let light and song be one.

Sing, like gleeful robins, clear and loud,
  When thy dreamy soul is summer-kisssed;
Be the smallest love-illumined cloud,
  Rather than the huge cold evening mist.

And may every heart that hears thy lays
  Sing in glad response, as mine has done.
Fly, sweet robin, on thy music ways;
  May the Brightest keep thee in the sun.

MOTHER NATURE.

    Oh! what a holy face
    Sweet Mother Nature wears!
Gentle and meek, and full of grace,
    Like the face of a soul at prayers,
While suns smile down from the answering skies,
And the wants of her heart exhale in sighs.

    Carefully, warily tread,
    Over the throbbing land;
For under your feet in many a bed
    Her embryo children stand;—
She covers them all from curious sight,
Till their sensitive eyes shall bear the light.

    Let your taste be ever so nice,
    Her minstrels will charm you long;
For she knoweth many a quaint device,
    To startle them into song;

She tutors them all — the sad, the gay —
Lest discord trouble the ear of day.

    Learn of her tender grace;
    For she hath learned of GOD.
She flings her arms, in a warm embrace,
    Over the dusky clod,
And, see! what wonderful things awake,
Out of the dark, for her sweet sake!

    Oh! anxious mothers, find,
    If ye can, her fairy gift;
Out of the yet untutored mind,
    All beautiful things to lift;
So shall your blooming children rise,
Pure in the light of your loving eyes.

THE STORY OF A WRONGED LIFE.

Over desert wilds she strayed,
   And the sand beneath was hot;
There was neither dewy shade,
   Pleasant glen, nor kindly grot.

Ah! so wearily she went,
   Burdened with her youth's lone years!
Strength and will alike were spent;
   All but faith was quenched in tears.

Lo! at length a garden fair
   Lay inviting by her side;
Pleasant fruits were blooming there,
   By cool rivers, deep and wide.

Presently, a face looked out;
   'Twas a pleasant, puzzling face;
But she had no heart to doubt,
   For the beauty of the place.

Sick and weary of the sand,
  Where her toiling feet had been,
Pleading, stretched she out her hand,
  And the Unknown led her in.

By the fountain's smiling side,
  By the fruit trees green and tall,
To the rivers cool and wide,
  Led her there, and that was all.

Famished, parched, the streams she eyed,
  And the fruit that hung so high;—
All her longing spirit cried,
  "Feed me, feed me, or I die!

"At the fountain let me quaff;
  See, its precious wave, how clear!"
Heard she then a taunting laugh—
  Saw she then a mocking sneer.

Sneers upon that puzzling face,
  Filled her soul with fear and doubt,—
From the pleasant, blooming place,
  Then the Unknown led her out.

'Twas the final drop of woe ;—
 Strength and will had gone before ;—
As she now, through wilds doth go,
 Faith walks with her never more.

THE HIDDEN FOUNTAIN.

Ho! brave knights! there's a mystic land
   Where sweet waters in melody flow;—
Who of all your valorous band
   Into its haunted verge will go?

There is a secret fountain there;—
   Precious gems in its pure waves lie;—
Pearls, that glimmer as soft and fair
   As the light of a smiling infant's eye.

Rubies, red as a rose's heart,
   Glow like a blush on the cheek of Truth.
And, whenever the ripples part,
   Diamonds flash like the eyes of youth.

Over this realm there reigns a queen—
   Fairest is she of all the fair—
Pass her by with a careless mien,
   Question her not if the fount is there.

She would lead thee a bootless chase,
    Laughing secretly all the while,
Bewildering thee with her changeful grace:—
    Ah! she is full of fairy guile.

Careless pass; yet arm thee, knight;—
    Well can the queen defend her own;—
Every glance of her eyes so bright,
    Straight at thy heart like a lance is thrown.

Well can the delicate, wayward maid,
    Ridicule's two-edged weapon wield;
Lest thou flee from its sweeping blade,
    Arm thyself with a brazen shield.

If taunts, like arrows, around thee fly,—
    Sarcasm's keenest shafts repel;
Strong thy heart, and thy bearing high,
    Press thou on to the hidden well.

Close to the fountain's banks of green,
    Blooms the delicate heliotrope,
And the saintly lily, a vestal queen,
    Lifts her pearl-white goblet up.

Timid violets bend their heads,
  Down by the blue-veined myrtle-blows,
Daisies peer from their lowly beds,
  Up at the buds of the blushing rose.

Ah! when once the fountain is found,
  Rich, brave knight, shall thy guerdon be;
Every gem of the haunted ground
  Gleams like a loving smile for thee.

Then shall the queen of this fairy land
  Whisper sweet blessings, in love's low tone;
Press to thy heart her dainty hand,
  Fountain and queen are all thine own.

Haste ye knights! or the hour will prove,
  All too late for your eager quest.
Who will search for the Fount of Love,
  Deep in the realm of a maiden's breast.

THE TRANSPLANTED FLOWER.

With the golden sunlight streaming
   O'er its little, blooming face,
Lay an infant, calmly dreaming,
   With a sweet, unconscious grace.

How I loved that cherub-creature,
   As he slept, so still and fair!
For each softly chiseled feature
   Seemed the seal of love to wear.

With the lilies drooping o'er him,
   And the daisies by his side,
And the streamlet just before him,
   With its gentle, murmuring tide;—

With a host of silken ringlets
   Crushed beneath the little head,
Still he lay, like sleeping fairy,
   Dreaming on the violet bed.

THE TRANSPLANTED FLOWER.

Close the chubby hands were folded
    O'er the little, beating heart;
And the lips, to beauty molded,
    Lay like poppy leaves apart;

While the breeze passed o'er him lightly,
    With a low and whispering sound,
And the sun was shining brightly
    On the meadows all around.

Not for worlds would I have wakened
    That sweet infant, slumbering there;
But I feasted on his beauty,
    And I breathed a silent prayer,

That the blight of sin should never
    Wither that bright opening flower,
Till, as pure and fresh as ever,
    It should grace a lovlier bower.

And that heartfelt prayer was granted;—
    Ere returning summer's reign,
The beauteous flower had been transplanted,
    And it bloomed in heaven again.

TO JENNIE K———.

A WATER-CURE FRIEND.

Oh! what will you do without me!
For my love for you, floats through the world
    of my breast,
As the zephyr of morning blows out of the west;
And your ear has been bowed for my blessing
    each day;
For love, sweet, is love, let it come whence it
    may;—
    Oh! what will you do without me?

Oh! what will you do without me,
To steal to your room, in the twilight-time,
With a pleasant tale, or a golden rhyme,
Or, low at your feet, to look up to your face,
And coax the thoughts out of their secret place?
    Now, what will you do without me?

Ah! what can you do without me?
You know you will wish for me morning and
  eve;
You know in the night you will waken and
  grieve;
For you said to me once, with a heavenly look,
"You open my heart as one opens a book;"
  So what can you do without me?

Nay! what shall I do without you?
Ah! vain, that I am! even now do I feel
Eclipses of loneliness over me steal,
And tremble to think of the wearisome days,
When we shall revolve in our separate ways;
  For what can I do without you?

Oh! what shall I do without you,
If the cold hand of sickness glide over each
  limb,
And my lids droop low, and mine eyes get
  dim,
And my voice quavers down to a gasping tone,
That is half a whisper and half a groan;—
  What then shall I do without you?

Oh! how can I live without you?
A face at my side, when I quivered with pain,
A voice stealing over my sensitive brain,
Saying, "Let me do this, for the sake of my love!"
This, this is the way it was wont to prove,
Oh! how can I live without you?

And yet I can live without you;
For when I have found a heart shaken and worn,
I will think of the cup of relief you have borne,
And I'll say, (all your beautiful actions to prove,)
"Drink, friend, of my draught, for the sake of my love;"
This way I can live without you.

A HYMN OF DEITY.

Sing, sing of the power of God; see where he flings
O'er his infant creation the shade of his wings;
While sun-warmed immensities under him lie,
And he writes his perfections on lily and sky.
    Sing, sing of his power—
Creator of planet, creator of flower.

Sing, sing of his justice, unchangeable, right;
Archangel and beggar are garbed with its light,
And the grass in the meadow is fashioned to wear
The crown of his brightness—the robe of his care.
    Sing, sing of the glow
Of his justice, that reaches so high and so low.

Sing, sing of his wisdom—a rule for the star
That rolls in its milk-white effulgence afar,
A wing for the bird—for the insect a plan—

A lair for the beast, and a spirit for man.
    Sing, sing of the broad,
And fatherly wisdom, the wisdom of God.

Sing, sing of his holiness, tender and sweet,
In the white, seventh heaven it glistens complete;
It shines on the world, in its night-shrouded place,
And the waves of humanity after it race.
    Sing, sing of the grace,
And ineffable purity lighting his face.

Sing, sing of his loves;—oh! sink down to your knees,
While ye sing of the grandeur, the sweetness of these;
Like ethereal tides, all the star-shores they lave;
They sanctify nature, they melt through the grave.
    Sing, sing of the sea,
Of his love, that is sweeping o'er you and o'er me.

Sing, sing of the Deity; softly and low
Let the rythmical pulses of melody flow;

While, like Christ at the river, he leans from the
 spheres,
For gratitude's holiest baptism — tears.
 Sing, sing till the dove,
Winging earthward, reveals the sweet course of
 his love.

Sing, sing! In his incomprehensible will,
He has made us, and loved us, and guarded us
 still.
We will carol his praises till death opes the
 door,
And leads us to sing at his feet evermore.
 Sing, sing till our sire,
Shall sweetly baptise us with holiest fire.

AND BEHOLD! IT WAS GOOD.

How grew this glad plant out of the ground?
   From the little seed that, long ago,
   Silent and humble, crept below,
Blind to the light and deaf to the sound,
   And, clasped to the breast of the nursing mold,
   From the deadly breath of the wintry cold,
A kindly and safe asylum found;

Then spring, like a cherishing Saviour stood,
   And opened its closed and sightless eyes,
   And touched its ears with exquisite cries,
And fed it with all nutritious food;
   Then it stirred in its vesture—stirred and grew
   Graceful of form and pleasant of hue,
And the smiling sun pronounced it good.

Compelled by mercy's silken bands,
 That clasped its warm and quivering limbs,
 It came, to join in worshipful hymns;
So, lifting its veined and beautiful hands,
 And waving its slow and gauzy wings,
 Among all happy created things,
Crowned with a fair, white flower, it stands.

How grew this great world out of space?
 From the nucleus seed, that, long ago,
 Dropped from the "tree of life" below,
And clasped in ether's kind embrace,
 Lay in a trance, till Deity came,
 And smiled upon it, and named its name,
And dewed it with all baptismal grace,

And fed it with warm electric food;
 Then it stirred in embryo life, and felt
 The frost of its wintry ages melt,
While the flame rushed through in a crimson
  flood,
 Quickening its senses, so obtuse,
 Sanctifying it to his use,
And the FATHER pronounced it very good.

'T was thus its tortuous course began,
   With cloud wings waving large, and far
   To follow the flight of the morning star,
And rivers of light beside it ran;
   So the bands of mercy this fair world lace,
   While it swings about in its radiant place,
And the flower wherewith it is crowned is man.

CAROLINE.

INSCRIBED TO MR. AND MRS. RICHARD JOHNSON,
AND N. M. TREADWELL.

How sad to see the human lie
　In the white coffin-room,
With marble breast that can not sigh,
　And cheek that may not bloom.

This calm, cold clay was Caroline.
　From 'neath this smooth lid's fall,
A gentle eye was wont to shine
　In kindliness on all.

These lips have spoken pleasant things;
　These stirless hands have moved
In such spontaneous care as brings
　A sense that we are loved.

These feet have walked with noiseless tread
　Beside you, hour by hour;

And on your arms this girlish head
   Has drooped like dew-weighed flower.

Ye weep for Carrie;—on her face
   Your briny teardrops fall,
And there their chilly courses trace;—
   She heeds them not at all.

Folded into the death-seas' flood,
   When late her gentle life
Had passed its princess maidenhood,
   And worn the crown of wife.

Out of her love-warm home she died,
   Just when another breast
Had drawn from her's its rippling tide,
   And woke to life's unrest.

Let the sweet rays of smiling day
   Steal round her, one by one,
Until we hide this cold, cold clay,
   Forever from the sun.

Alas! that death's white vail should sweep
   Across her placid brow!
Weep for doubly wedded, weep!
   The "Bride of Heaven" now.

Pass on toward the grave! ye know
   This is not Caroline.
Where she has gone, we too shall go;
   Both your freed souls and mine.

Weep, weep no more! for death's white vail,
   If lifted, in the place
Of this calm cheek, so cold and pale,
   Would show an angel's face.

SPRING WINDS.

The spring winds wander deftly,
   At work the live-long hours,
Shaking the green stems softly,
   And coaxing out the flowers.

Drifting aside with laughter
   The leaves so old and brown,
That sulky autumn's sobbing,
   With sighing breath, blew down.

Lifting into the sunshine
   The timid wind-flower's head,
And piling up green mosses,
   About the sun-dew's bed.

Brushing the rust of winter
   From nature's golden lute,
Touching the strings in prelude,
   While summer's voice is mute.

Spreading the fern's green mantle
  Above the covering forms,
Of little bind-weed blossoms,
  That tremble at the storms.

So the spring winds walk deftly,
  At work the live-long hours,
Shaking the green stems softly,
  And coaxing out the flowers.

Thus, when the heart's dark winter
  With chilling wind has gone,
Who would not be the zephyr,
  To hasten summer on?

When little words of kindness
  Such thrills of joy confer,
Who would not set the heart-strings,
  With melody astir.

Spring wind, at work so deftly,
  About the scented grove,
Well dost thou teach that kindness
Can but awaken love!

For gentle, soft embraces,
And tender smiling eyes,
Dispel the darkest storm-clouds
That hurtle through the skies.

THE WORLD.

Why should I weep for the world?
   Weeping would never avail,
To wring from his ruthless breast a sigh,
   Or loosen his coat of mail.

Who to his lofty head,
   Or his bragging lip would trust?
For, still, with a giant's mighty tread,
   He tramples us into the dust.

Why for his smile should I pine?
   What can he give to me?
Gold from the depth of the hard-worked mine?
   Pearls from the rolling sea?

Nay! but he gives not these;
   And if he did, what then?

Neither the wealth of land or seas
  Maketh the wealth of men.

Many a man, whose chest
  Locketh the shining gold,
Knows of a room, within his breast,
  Empty, and dark, and cold.

What are his blooming lands,
  What are his money-bags,
When, in the night of death, he stands,
  A beggarly soul in rags?

And if to the world I kneel
  What will he give me then?
Flowery wreaths for my spirit's weal?
  Loves of women and men?

Nay; for the brightest flowers
  Wither along his path;
And every soul with its loves and powers
  Weareth his sign of scath.

Oh! beggarly world, depart!
  Thou hast not a gift for me;

Tears come out of my sorrowing heart;
  But I am not weeping for thee.

Only for those who trust,
  World, in thy fleeting charms;
Weeping, to see them fall like dust
  Out of thy nerveless arms.

Oh! semblance of wealth and worth,
  Where is thy boasted might?
Canst thou not gather thy lovers forth,
  Out of the realm of night?

Nay? then, thou world, depart!
  For I have in my soul, to-day,
A treasure, to which thy golden mart
  Is but a pit of clay.

Here, here in my heart, there lies
  A palace of beauty rare;
And sweet, white faces and holy eyes
  Look pleasantly on me there.

Those angels—sweet prophets are they—
  Singing ballads of heavenly bliss;

Oh, world! with thy glittering pageants gay,
　Thou givest me nothing like this.

Thou callest thyself a king.
　Go, monarch, and leave me alone;
For an adder-coil is thy signet ring,
　And a sepulchre thy throne.

THE SOUL'S TRIUMPH.

Come in, oh, my visitor, Sorrow,
    Come into my heart for a while;
Let me see if thine eyes can not borrow
    Some light from the sun of my smile.

The May waltzes over the meadow,
    The little birds carol in tune;
What news from the region of shadow?
    Are clouds floating up for my June?

"Oh! soul! the bright castle of wonders,
    Built up in thine April delight,
Is rocked by reality's thunders,
    And fades, like thin mist, out of sight!

It is well;—for the structure was airy,
    And frail, as a castle could seem;—
Its halls were but fit for a fairy;
    Its pillars were hewn of a dream.

Let it pass, with its perishing glory—
    The toy of a baby at best—
Small heed has thy dolorous story,
    When May blisses sing in my breast!

Art thou come again, visitor Sorrow?
    How white is thy face, and how thin!
Come thou to my June bower, and borrow,
    The bloom and the luster within.

The summer sun laughs in the azure,
    The gleeful winds laugh in the trees;
And full of its youth and its pleasure,
    My light heart is laughing with these.

"Nay, soul! for a pallor is creeping
    Across the blue heaven of bliss;
Disease opes the fountains of weeping;
    The mirth of thy laugh is amiss."

Now, skeleton fetters have bound me;
    Yet they are but fetters of clay,
And, warmed with the sunshine around me,
    I yet can be smiling and gay.

THE SOUL'S TRIUMPH.

The loves of the human shall feed me,
   Like droppings of honeycomb dew;—
The rose-links of beauty shall lead me,
   And autumn hang grapes in my view.

Again dost thou enter, oh, Sorrow?
   Thy dark robe is faded and torn.
Hast thou come in thy squalor, to borrow
   These garments of light I have worn?

I yield thee my August tiara,
   And take the full cup thou dost bear;—
It is brimming with waters of Marah —
   What news from the land of despair?

" Wail, soul! for the frowning September
   Has hewn down thy loves to their graves;
Already the cruel November
   His scepter of dreariness waves."

Now, dark is the earthly, the outer;
   And icy my lusterless bower;
But shall I turn, trembler, and doubter,
   The football of fear, from this hour?

I will close up the door of my dwelling,
    And light up the fire on the hearth;—
My songs to the world shall be telling,
    All night, of my banquet of mirth.

Once more, oh, dark prophetess, Sorrow!
    Come into the house of my heart;
Let me see if thy form can not borrow
    Some warmth, ere I bid thee depart.

The light and the beauty are faded;
    The gladness and glory are o'er;
Life's butterfly wings are abraded;—
    What news from the Stygian shore?

"Oh! soul, as I passed through the valley,
    Where blackness hangs down like a weight,
I saw the fleet death-armies rally,
    And, lo! they are at thy gate."

Now, Sorrow, thy name shall be Sorrow
    No more, while eternities roll!
Thou dost promise a brighter to-morrow
    Than ever yet gladdened my soul.

The death-armies move at the pleasure
  Of one who is mighty to save.
The sun smiles again in the azure,
  And flowers droop over the grave.

Dost thou see not the mansion of wonders,
  Built up for my sky-climbing feet?
It is rocked by no terrible thunders,
  Nor smitten by simoon or sleet.

And seest thou my golden tiara,—
  My glistening garment of white?
Oh! sweet are the waters of Marah!
  And, Sorrow, thy name is Delight!

The loves of the cherubim feed me,
  Like droppings of honeycomb dew;
To their warm, lustrous bowers they lead me;
  I wither — to blossom anew.

A WINTER IN SPRING.

How frosty and bare seems the world, love!
    I am sorrowing all the while;
For I miss the warm blaze of thine earnest eye,
    And the bloom of thy beautiful smile.

There's a blank in my life and my heart, love,
    That ought to be filled by thee.
I have waited and watched so long, love—
    Why comest thou not to me?

The bird is seeking his mate, love;
    The breezes are kissing the flowers;
There is union of other dear hearts, love—
    Why is there no union of ours?

The wavelets are singing their songs, love,
    At the feet of the flowers on the shore;

A WINTER IN SPRING.

But the voice that once caroled to me, love,
   Is caroling to me no more.

I bend me over my books, love,
   From yearning my spirit to free;
But they can not conceal the bright looks, love,
   That used to beam kindly on me.

The poet is only a poet;
   The sage is only a sage;
But thy voice would furnish the heart, love,
   To speak to me out of the page.

Hast thou said that my friendship was false, love?
   Oh, who could be faithless to thee!
Then send me but one little word, love,
   How trifling soever it be.

One word, just to say that you're well, love,
   And happy—I'll ask for no more;
And I'll treasure it up in my heart, love,
   Where I've treasured so many before.

For I sigh, as I look from my window,
   And watch the bright birds where they swing.

This silence, this dreary neglect, love,
   Have made a dull winter of spring.

Return, oh, my light-hearted maiden!
   And shine through my cloud-shadowed hours.
They wait but thy song and thy sunlight
   To blossom all out into flowers.

SUMMER.

To-day, my soul discerned
  A measure, solemn and slow,
That came, and went, and back returned,
  Like waves in ebb and flow.

The world lies sad and lone
  Under a wintry day;
But thou hast a summer coming on,
  That never shall pass away.

Pain of thy brow and heart,
  Hours of weeping and strife;
These are the things that have made thee smart
  Under a wintry life.

But sorrow can not intrude
  In the smile of thy coming hours;
Then beautiful thoughts, all wise and good,
  Will bloom in thy soul like flowers.

The darkened valley is near;
  But be thou brave and strong;
For, lo! at the end the light is clear,
  And the way can not be long.

Let the swift seasons march
  With glooms and glories by;
While over them all is bowed the arch
  Of the blue, majestic sky.

A summer or two may lean
  Over thy stranded boat;
A winter or two will glide between,
  And then it will surely float.

The cowering world must lie
  Under its wintry day;
But a summer waits for the soul, on high,
  That never shall pass away.

My listening spirit knows
  The truth of the solemn lay;
I pause, as the measure comes and goes,
  And I lift my heart to pray.

"Oh! open the gates so bright,
  Where lingers the shining band!
Let through to my soul the floods of light
  That roll in the spirit land!"

Sweet tears to my eyelids start,
  At thought of my wondrous gain;
For I soon shall love with an angel's heart,
  And think with an angel's brain.

IF.

If I ever love you,
(As, perchance, I may,)
'T will be when I prove you
True in all you say.
Faithful-hearted, ardent, kind,
High of soul, and pure of mind;
Be all this, and you shall know
How a woman's love may grow,
Like the new-moon, small and white,
Broadening to a full-orbed light.

If I ever serve you,
(Served by you in turn,)
Happy if I nerve you
For life's conflict stern,
'T will be when I know you brave,
Grateful for the good you crave,
Strong in energy and will,

Merciful and careful still,
Moved by trouble's lightest call,
Loving many, helping all.

  If I ever nourish
  As the ground the plant,
  Blessed if you but flourish
  Though my life be scant,
'T will be when I see you bear
Deeds, like flowers, complete and fair,
Of all worthy purpose born,
Hedged not with the mocking thorn.
Oh! I could not bear to be
Tender of the thistle-tree.

  If I learn to bless you,
  (Blest your life to share,)
  Lingering to caress you,
  With a silent prayer,
For the sweet continuance
Of our love's serene romance,
'T will be when my soul receives
Knowledge where it now believes.
Only what I think you, prove,
And I give you love for love.

MY SPIRIT LUTE.

I have a little spirit lute —
   A lute that's all my own;
Whose treasured melodies are heard
   By my fond heart alone.

Yet, others play that lute, and oh!
   Of all I ever knew,
None ever touched its golden chords,
   But worthy friends and true.

And, if I guard my spirit lute
   From every touch profane,
Never along its chords shall ring
   One sharp, discordant strain.

To "Vinnie" one sweet chord I yield,
   And she can make, at will,
The richest, deepest melody
   Along my heart-strings thrill.

And "Mae" can touch one golden string,
    So sweetly, and so well,
"Mae," or an angel, which it is,
    Sometimes, I can not tell.

And from my viewless spirit lute,
    One chord I love to lend
To Ellen, dear, true-hearted girl,
    My loved, and faithful friend.

Jeannette, whose cheerful, winning smile,
    Is yet undimmed by sadness,
Can wake, in my unquiet soul,
    Sweet tones of hope and gladness.

Dear, merry-hearted cousin, "Liss,"
    Can wake the gayest strain,
And ease my weary, yearning heart,
    Of more than half its pain.

And like the light and dainty song
    Of some sweet woodland fairy,
Gushes the music of the chord,
    That's played by gentle "Carrie."

And there is one — shall nameless be —
  Whose lip in death is mute,
Who used to wake wild music o'er
  My viewless spirit lute.

And yet, I have another friend,
  Whose name I can not tell;
Nor know I in what distant clime
  My unknown friend doth dwell.

But if my heart has sung aright,
  When my poor life is told,
Then, hand in hand, my friend and I
  Shall walk the streets of gold.

Then to that truest spirit friend,
  I'll yield my spirit lute,
Eternally its strains shall blend,
  And not a chord be mute.

A PHANTASY.

*"Know ye the land of love?
Its ancient boundaries? the broad extent
Of its illimitable continent?"*

When stars without number
  Lit twilight's broad breast,
And gleamings of umber
  Lay low in the west,
I found in my slumber
  The land of the blest.

Oh! sweet was my dreaming!
  With surgings of light,
My vailed brain was teeming,
  Albeit 't was night;
With mystical seeming,
  Creation was white.

All times were light leisures,
Delicious, complete;

A PHANTASY.

My thoughts ran to measures,
  As water songs sweet;
All flowery treasures
  Grew under my feet.

I felt like the palmer,
  On holiest plain.
All turbulent clamor,
  All babblings vain,
Were lost in the glamour
  That curtained my brain.

Sweet land of the loving,
  So drowsily white,
Where glad wings were moving
  In murmurous flight,
And rivers were grooving
  The valley-land bright!

O, rapturous being,
  Where melody flew,
Each swift strain agreeing
  With symphonies new,
Like trooping birds fleeing
  In parallels true!

I dreamed — and I waken; —
   I dreamed but an hour; —
My joys are down-shaken
   Like dews from a flower;
But dews are retaken,
   And dreams have a power.

So, when I grow eager
   For riddance of pain,
When doubtings beleaguer
   My laboring brain,
And love feasts are meager,
   I'll slumber again.

BELL.

Where is little Bell?
The flowers in yonder darkened dell,
    As pale as moonlight, stand,
To wait the plucking by the hand
    Of tiny, smiling Bell.

    She was akin to those;—
Her face was like a fair, wild rose;—
    Her liquid, sparkling eyes,
Were like two dewdrops of the skies,
    Let down at daylight's close.

    Where is laughing Bell?
The streamlet where she loved so well
    To sit and dream, of yore,
Climbs nimbly up its grass-grown shore,
    To watch for pretty Bell.

    She was akin to that;
For still her merry, rippling chat

Flowed through us all the day;
And thoughts as sweet as flowers of May
   Within our hearts begat.

   Where is beauteous Bell?
The birds whose songs were wont to swell
   In greeting, when she came,
Seem softly saying o'er her name,
   And asking, "Where is Bell?"

   Her voice was wont to be
Brimful of pleasant melody,—
   Not learned, but always known,
And gurgling out in every tone,
   Delicious, clear, and free.

   Where is gentle Bell?
The hearts that prisoned her so well,
   Are rifled of their love;—
The fluttering pinions of the dove
   Flew out, O, where is Bell?

   The little drawer is piled
With her small garments, white and undefiled,
   And somewhere underneath
The barren clay, there lies a bed of death,—
   There sleeps the child!

SNOW-BERRIES.

PART I.

If I, by a magic power,
Pluck the sweet rose of the olden time;
That rose, that was withered before its prime,
   Wilt thou dew, with thy tears, the flower?

Can it bloom as of old, to-day?
Let us look for the honey of love, and see
If passing distrust, like a ravishing bee,
   Has stolen it all away.

The night is with me again!
When I heard, for the first, thy soft voice in
     the air,
In dulcet quavers of merriment rare,
   That captured the dullest brain.

I watched thy smiling face,
Drifting along the human flood;

And saw, where, after the smile, there stood
A black robed woe in its place.

I heard them, whispering, say,
"She is changeful and wild as an April hour;"
And I said, "From her sepulchred heart, no power
Rolled ever the stone away."

But they answered, "She has thrown
The loves of those who would love aside;—
Her soul is full of a willful pride;
She is selfish — let her alone."

Away from me thou did'st glide,
With a light, low laugh, dividing the crowd;
But I heard, in the laugh, a wailing loud —
The surge of love's refluent tide.

Plenteous, pure, and sweet,
A rill gushed out of my own heart's rock,
That gathered its waves in a silver flock,
And flung them at thy feet.

Oh! I did love thee, Mae!
Loved thee, — as nightingales love the night —

As the lone cloud loves the full moon white —
  As orioles love the day.

  If thou didst chance to frown,
And turn away from my proffered lips,
It was to me as a frost that nips
  The loveliest lilies down.

  And, when thy frown was lost
In a sunrise smile, sweetly flooding thy face,
My lilies bloomed with a brighter grace,
  I said, for the cruel frost.

  Witness the ardent lines
I sent to thy heart, articulate
With the lore of love, as wind tunes mate
  With the words of the odorous pines!

Witness the angry light
That burned in my eyes, when they blamed
  thee so,
For the madness of one whose brain with woe
  Had sunk from its manly hight!

  Witness the tears I shed,
When thou didst for love's sweet sake, uncover

Thy hopes, from the shroud that wrapped them
   over,
  To show me thy beautiful dead!

  Witness them all—I loved!
But the wildest gleam of my childhood glee,
Though it rose and fell like the star on the sea,
  Was firm as thy friendship proved.

  What robbed my cherishing heart
Of the exquisite bliss of thy clinging love?
Alas! that a viewless thing could move
  Our coupled spirits apart!

  The sea of our love was high;
And linked together, like shallops light,
We moved in the wind, like birds in flight;—
  I looked, and thou wert not nigh.

  Why do the years return,
And open their gloomiest walks to-day?
I can but linger awhile, and pray
  Over each shattered urn.

  It can but give me pain
To see the shut buds of my fickle spring;

But the vines of thy dead love round me cling,
  And fetter me like a chain.

And memory starts from her sleep,
While I lean from my storm-toss'd ark, and yearn
For Mae, the flown dove of my soul to return,
  Before I am whelmed in the deep.

Or ever my heart shall know
The chill that heralds the awful grave —
I pause at the wintry drift, and crave
  A flower, ere my head lies low.

And I would that thou shouldst see,
Over the cold snow's shrouding robes,
A light stem, drooping with milk-white globes,
  The fruit of my knowledge of thee.

For the love in the summer born,
Only within two girlish souls,
Like plants, upspringing in fragile bowls,
  In one of them lives unshorn.

My darling, it will not die;
But circles the fuller — the more complete —

However thou rack'st it with wind and sleet,
   Than under the summer sky.

There cometh a time full fast,
On earth, or in heaven, I may not say,
When thou wilt gather these heart-fruits, Mae,
   And cherish them all, at last.

PART II.

There are times when the soul doth lean
Down toward the valley from whence it hath climbed,
To listen once more for the dirges that chimed
   From the bitter waters between.

There are hours when it seems to know
That a raven is flying up from the vale,
And nerves itself for a sorrowful tale,
   With a prescient song of woe.

I had hardly sung my lay,
When there came a message to me, that said,
"The bride of a month lies stricken and dead;
   The maiden whose name was Mae."

And this is why, when I wrote,
"Thou wilt gather these heart-fruits soon," I heard,
The chime of a sweet, assenting word,
  Out of the blue sky float.

Oh! Mae! beloved of my heart!
That thou shouldst have lifted thy spirit-wings,
Floating out of the shroud of perishing things,
  When we were so far apart!

Oh! that thou hadst told me why
Thou didst treat my love as a useless thing,
And toss it away, as one might fling
  A pearl, that is tear-dimmed, by!

I had thought to lose my breath
Or ever thou didst, for my lamp burned dimly;
And I knew I should see what stood so grimly
  Between us, after the death.

With a desperate will to cloke
The love I never had cloked before,
I thought, if the thrill of my heart-strings is o'er,
  They shall be like the sinews of oak.

It may be, a slandering lip
Sent a false tale into thy sensitive ear,
That tingled with echoing faith to hear
   The lash of the scorpion whip.

And if I had said, "But prove
That I have done aught to forfeit thy heart,"
I had seen the dark cloud of thine anger depart,
   And let down the star of thy love.

But wo for the stubborn pride,
Closing my lips that I could not brook
To ask for a smile, or a tender look,
   Though, lacking it, I had died!

For, just as my ice-bound soul
Had broken the links that had fettered it long,
And I said, "I will call back her love with a song,"
   Then, then did the death-bell toll.

And the long procession of woes
Crept down from my eyes at the solemn sound,
While I laid my head on the frosty ground,
   And sighed for the blasted rose,

Saying, "Now, by my sobbing breath,
By the misery racking my smitten heart,
I will play nevermore this cowardly part,
  Till my loves are buried in death.

"For, 'few are the days of our years,'
And love is the only light we have
To paint us the splendor beyond the grave —
  The rainbow over the tears.

"Oh, beautiful April child!
Oh, glorified spirit! lean out of the skies,
And warm my cold heart with the sun of thine
    eyes;
  For the winter is dreary and wild!

"And I ask for a smile to day,
While I linger under the cypress tree,
And sweep my harp in a dirge for thee,
  My angel love, my Mae."

IN MEMORIAM.

The winds go sobbing their prayerful masses,
  Wanting the sound of thy laughter sweet;

The dumb earth yearns into asking grasses,
  Missing the tread of thy dancing feet.

Thy sisters look into each other's faces,
  Pale for the ghost of a presence fled;
Thy lover hides him in secret places,
  To think of his bride, trampled down with the dead.

Thy mother looks from her shaded casement,
  With an anguish couched in her dim, deep eyes,
And cowers at thy tomb in bitter abasement,
  With a robe and a heart like the midnight skies.

Thy friends who were false — and their name is legion —
  Talk with smooth words of thee, now thou art dead;
But thou hearest them not in the soundless region,
  Where thou hast pillowed thy graceful head.

Full of the keen, cold wind of trouble,
  From breath to breath careening about,

Thou didst soar, at last, like a gilded bubble,
　Just when the love-bright sun shone out.

A wall of clay and a grave-stone guard thee.
　My song dies away in an under-breath;
For my river of love, as it leaps toward thee,
　Stiffens to ice in the presence of Death.

THE DEAD PINE.

In the center of the wood,
    Where a little clearing lay,
A sequestered dwelling stood,
    Waiting for my feet, one day.

Coming in, a road cut out
    Through the berry brambles, led;
Winding curiously about,
    O'er the rough, root-matted bed.

Full five hundred years, or more,
    Had been training up the pines;
All along the forest floor,
    Marshaling them in stately lines.

Redly flamed the autumn sun;
    And, upon the eddying air,
Came the torn leaves, one by one—
    Some were dusky, some were fair.

Maples, lithe and crimson leaved,
   Leaning earthward, touched my cheek;
And the drooping beeches grieved,
   As if just about to speak.

But the tales they would have told,
   By the minstrel pines were caught,
And in mystic language rolled
   Downward for my solving thought.

Language "eerie" soft and strange,
   And I listened with a thrill;
Did it breathe of earthly change,
   Or of something sadder still?

Must I, in this secret place,
   See my life-hopes torn away,
As the pines, with solemn face,
   Saw the forest leaves, that day?

Who could tell? but this I knew,
   Surely as the world doth roll,
I must have my autumn, too,
   Chilling all my stricken soul.

Fresh from city sound and sight,
   Bowed I then my head and sighed.
With a sadness half delight,
   And a gladness tearful-eyed.

"Here, a little while," I said,
   "Will I linger to prepare
For the dwellings of the dead,
   For the gloom and silence there.

"Gathering from the sweeping wind,
   Gathering from the waving trees,
Sweet delights to feed the mind
   Or a crowd of miseries.

"Calm seclusion well may suit
   Those who feel the life-pulse fail;
Birds, whose latest songs are mute,
   Ended in a broken wail.

"It is very sad," I said,
   "But, when sickness stays the flight,
Though we live, we yet are dead,
   In the morning, crowned with night."

Standing in the cabin door,
   When the evening hours were gone,
Three most lofty pines before,
   Singing in the crimson dawn.

Then I saw, not far away,
   One that had been dead so long,
That the rising wind of day
   Could not rouse it into song.

"Oh, most bitter lot!" I thought,
   "Thus to stand, unthrilled and mute,
When all else is music-fraught,
   Like the breath within the flute.

"Silent, melancholy tree,
   Saddest feelings thou dost bring
Am I not akin to thee —
   I, who nevermore can sing?"

And a pity in my heart,
   For the heart of that dead pine,
Grew, until it seemed to start
   Into something more divine.

More divine than it could be,
  Being dead, unfruitful, cold;
In its youth, a simple tree —
  Nothing, now that it was old.

Oh! the heart will bud and bloom
  Into little loves like this —
Loves that hover round a tomb,
  Images of death to kiss.

Every morning, thus I stood,
  Looking past the stately three,
Where, beside the withered wood,
  Towered my blasted, songless tree.

Every evening, thus I said,
  "Ere another dawn shall break,
We who live, and yet are dead,
  In the final blast may quake."

Once, at night, I woke, and high
  Raved the winter's voice of fear;
Tempests rode along the sky,
  Wind-wails sounded in my ear.

Strangely startled where I lay,
    Looking southward, through the glass,
I could see, along their way,
    All the cloudy legions pass.

Oh! the mad, beseeching signs!
    Oh! the long, despairing call!
Oh! the surging of the pines,
    Like a roaring waterfall.

"Such are we," I murmured low,
    "Mocked of life and racked with pain;
Struck by all the winds that blow;
    Crying out for help in vain."

While my fierce rebellion grew
    Strong, tempestuous as the wind,
Sudden sounds came in, and drew
    Outwardly my striving mind.

Something like a woful shriek;
    Something like a hurried blow;
Then a gasping cry, and weak;
    Then an instant overthrow.

THE DEAD PINE.

Ah! no more, my blasted tree,
   Brother of my heart and life,
Will I look at morn on thee —
   Ended evermore the strife.

Leaning toward my window-pane,
   By the dawning's earliest line
Came a wonder to my brain —
   Stood unbowed my blasted pine;

But of those — the stately three —
   One green head was stricken low;
And there came a thought to me,
   While I smiled to see it so.

"When the grief-wind, full of dread,
   Raves around the human heart,
We who live, and yet are dead,
   Are not they who feel the smart.

"But some life that never wore
   Sign of scath, or scar of wound,
Smitten to its very core,
   Wailing, dying, seeks the ground."

Once, again. The day was laid
    At the noontide in a shroud;
And the woodman's labor made
    All the air with echoes loud.

Talking, by the firelight-shine,
    Some one, entering, said to me,
"Soon will fall your blasted pine;
    Hurry to the door and see!"

Leaning outward, in the cold,
    Then I whispered, with a sigh,
"Of what use the sick and old?
    Brother of my heart, good by.

"Blows, resounding, sharp and fast,
    Through the clearing, smite my ear.
Brother, once the cleaving past,
    Thou and I have nought to fear."

Suddenly, by impulse new,
    As if something told me so,
Turned I to the stately two,
    Looking for the overthrow.

Instantly the axe grew still;
   And I saw the loftiest wave,
Just a little, from the hill,
   As if looking for a grave.

Slowly, slowly, slowly bowed,
   Struggling, with a giant strength,
From its dwelling, 'mid the cloud,
   Came the noble head at length.

Oh, the quivering! the strain,
   Tugging at each fibre fine;
Oh, the yearning cries of pain!
   Oh, the falling of the pine!

With a sound of rushing power,
   With a last, unearthly call,
Broken, like a fragile flower,
   Lay the stateliest tree of all.

Leaning outward, in the cold,
   "Brother of my heart," I said,
" Who would smite the sick or old?
They who live and yet are dead.

"We the work of time must wait,
　While the slow years round us creep,
Ere we yield us to our fate,
　Quickly crumbling down to sleep."

Now, the fair, white-handed May,
　Like a gentle nurse, came near,
Where the sick world moaning lay,
　And she smiled away his fear.

Touched his pulses, faint and low;
　Stirred his heart-strings, still and weak.
Till the life, in sudden flow,
　Ran along his swarthy cheek.

Rambling o'er the blossoming ground,
　I, with infantile delight,
Some new glory ever found,
　Waiting for my happy sight.

But, one morn, upon the hill,
　Loitering in the joy of day,
Some weird feeling seemed to fill
　All my soul with sore dismay.

Soon a low and groaning sound,
  Now afar, and now a-near,
Seemed to trail along the ground,
  Lifting then to touch my ear.

This way, that way, did I look,
  Nothing strange was in my sight:
But the brake-fronds near me shook,
  And the birds came down from flight.

Then, a crackling, crumbling noise—
  "Ah!" I said, "my blasted pine,
When all else is rocked with joys,
  Saddest fate must now be thine."

But there came a horrid crash;
  In the fair face of the sun
There was made a sudden gash—
  Earthward swept the stately one.

Green, and flourishing, and strong,
  Yet some fibre underneath,
Like a lute-string strained too long,
  Parting, let it down to death.

Then I sat me down to think;
  For my lonely, songless tree
Stood above the streamlet brink,
  Looking down upon the three.

"If the tempest-grief go by,
  If misfortune's weapon spare,
They who thrive may sink and die,
  Like this pine, when all is fair.

"In the largest life and thought,
  Death may claim his human prey;
And the flesh with vigor fraught,
  Pales and turns but common clay.

"But, alas! oh, brother, old!
  We who live and yet are dead,
Wait the night and wintry cold —
  These must end our doom of dread."

———

Never came the hectic blush
  To a lady's pleasant face,
Softlier than the crimson flush,
  Tinting every wooded place.

Never sunk a lady's tone
  To a more melodious fall,
Than the dying summer's moan,
- While she waited for the pall.

Now, within the cabin door,
  With a heavy heart and eye,
Outwardly I leaned once more,
  Looking toward earth and sky.

"Oh! most quiet home of mine,
  Linked so tightly to my heart,
Give me now some farewell sign,
  Ere my loitering feet depart.

"Back to city sound and sight,
  Some new lesson let me bear,
That shall teach my soul aright
  Both to suffer and to dare.

"Not a song upon the wind,
  And the sunset in the west —
So must evening shroud the mind!
  So must silence seal the breast!

"Oh! thou blasted, songless pine!
　Thou, whose day will surely end,
Well I named thee, brother mine!
　To a common night we tend."

While I lifted up my eyes,
　To its lofty top there came,
Straightway, from the far off skies
　Sudden lines of golden flame.

Now, my brother seemed to wear
　Such a halo round his head,
That no more my lips could dare
　Call the stately prophet dead.

In his majesty he stood,
　Glorified before my sight;—
Of the broad, encircling wood,
　Only he, was crowned with light.

"Now, perchance," I wondering said,
　"He some other life may claim
And this silence, like the dead,
　Bear significance the same.

"Surely, soul has such large springs,—
   Is so infinite in scope,
Even dull, insentient things,
   May have spirit-life to hope.

"From the Father's breast, a vein
   Reaches down to every heart.
May we not send out again,
   Of our life some little part?

"If a globule of our love
   Beat against a tree or flower,
Does it not begin to move,
   Even with a soul that hour?

"Why does sunset crown the pine,
   That is dead, if not to show
That its heart, as well as mine,
   Yet will triumph over woe?

"Coming out of midnight wind;—
   Coming out of wintry strife,
Leaving 'living death' behind,
   In the realm of dying life.

"And who knows but when in me
  Spirit-life shall sweetly thrive,
I shall find this stately tree,
  By my loving made alive?

"While the sunrise flames shall play
  All around us, brother mine,
We may both be named that day,
  Songful soul, and songful pine."

Who the simple thought can blame?
  For when sunset ends the day,
Every thing is touched with flame,
  Even to the sordid clay.

And my life-sun, being low,
  Falling o'er this blasted pine,
Made it seem, beneath the glow,
  Something larger — more divine.

More divine than it could be,
  Being dead, unfruitful, cold;
In its youth, a simple tree —
  Nothing, now that it was old.

Still, thereafter, when I turned
    Backward, for a farewell gaze,
All my heart within me burned,
    Like the hearts of August days.

Smiling at my little thought,
    "Yet," I said, "Oh, prophet tree!
Thou hast many a lesson taught —
    Silent, though thou art — to me.

"If a globule of our love
    Beat against a tree or flower,
We ourselves begin to move,
    With a larger soul, that hour.

"But the earthly can not be
    Lit with aught but transient flames.
Songful soul, and songless tree —
    God himself shall name the names.

"When I spread my wings in flight —
    When my feet have spurned the clay,
I shall whisper, 'One, at night,
    Did prefigure this my day.'

"One insensient, still, and cold,
   Lifting up his head on high,
Showed me how the sick and old
   Catch the splendors of the sky.

"Being bare of leaves, the wind
   Passes by, with scarce a blow;
Being sapless, none can find
   Reason for an overthrow.

"Being all unthrilled and mute,
   Death, who makes the heart-strings quake,
As a rough hand strikes a lute,
   Can not find a chord to break.

"It is very sweet," I said,
   "When dark sickness stays the flight,
We may live, though we are dead;
   In the eve be crowned with light.

"Autumn prophesies of spring;
   Sunset prophesies of morn;
And the silent lip will sing
   When the soul is newly born.

www.ingramcontent.com/pod-product-compliance
Lightning Source LLC
Chambersburg PA
CBHW022100230426
43672CB00008B/1230